CBT vs NLP: Which is right for me?

Rewiring Your Brain with Cognitive Behavioral Therapy vs Neuro-Linguistic Programming. How To Get in Control of Your Behaviors and Emotions (Neuroscience Guide)

Written by Derick Parsons

© **Copyright 2019 Derick Parsons - All rights reserved.**

The content contained within this book may not be reproduced, duplicated or transmitted without direct written permission from the author or the publisher.

Under no circumstances will any blame or legal responsibility be held against the publisher, or author, for any damages, reparation, or monetary loss due to the information contained within this book. Either directly or indirectly.

Legal Notice:

This book is copyright protected. This book is only for personal use. You cannot amend, distribute, sell, use, quote or paraphrase any part, or the content within this book, without the consent of the author or publisher.

Disclaimer Notice:

Please note the information contained within this document is for educational and entertainment purposes only. All effort has been executed to present accurate, up to date, and reliable, complete information. No warranties of any kind are declared or implied. Readers acknowledge that the author is not engaging in the rendering of legal, financial, medical or professional advice. The content within this book has been derived from various sources. Please consult a licensed professional before attempting any techniques outlined in this book.

By reading this document, the reader agrees that under no circumstances is the author responsible for any losses, direct or indirect, which are incurred as a result of the use of information contained within this document, including, but not limited to, — errors, omissions, or inaccuracies.

Table of Contents

Introduction 7

Chapter 1: Definitions 11

  What is Cognitive Behavioral Therapy (CBT)?11

    What Is the Origin of CBT? 16

  What Is Neuro-Linguistic Programming (NLP)? 30

    What Is the Origin of NLP? 34

Chapter 2: How To Practice 70

  How To Practice CBT 70

    With a Therapist 70

    By Yourself 79

  How To Practice NLP 82

    With a Professional 82

    Practicing NLP By Yourself 88

Chapter 3: Examples of Techniques 92

  6 CBT Techniques 92

    Calm Breathing 92

    Realistic Thinking 94

- Pleasant Activity Scheduling 98
- Progressive Muscle Relaxation (PMR) 100
- Exposure 104
- Mindfulness 107

6 NLP Techniques 113
- Meta Model 114
- Anchoring 128
- Representational System Discovery 133
- Perceptual Positions 135
- Rapport 143
- Swish Pattern 146

Chapter 4: Benefits 151

What are CBT's Main Benefits? 151
- Cognitive Distortions 151

What are NLP's Main Benefits? 170
- Psychological Issues 170
- Performance at Work 177

Chapter 5: CBT vs. NLP 182

The Main Differences Between CBT and NLP 182
- Problem-Oriented vs. Growth-Oriented ... 182

 Conscious vs. Unconscious 183
 High Need for Individual's Input vs. Low Need for Individual's Input 184

The Main Similarities Between CBT and NLP 185
 Focus on Changing Dysfunctional Thinking Patterns 185
 Focus on Perception of Events Instead of the Actual Events 186
 Focus on the Present and not the Past 186
 Putting the Responsibility on the Individual 187

 CBT or NLP: Which One is Right For You? . 188

Conclusion 194

References 197

Introduction

Hello, reader! My name is Meg, I am 34 years old, and I am from London, United Kingdom. For a while now, I have been studying the numerous types of therapy there are. With so much variety in the industry and with so many human beings in the world whose brains function in completely different ways, whose previous experiences are completely different and whose struggles might be of all kinds, I find that it is not only extremely interesting but also important for people to be aware of what choices they have. This becomes even more important when we consider that according to the House of Commons Library, in 2018, 1 in 6 people from the United Kingdom experienced some kind of common mental disorder on the week before they were questioned[1]; or that, according to the World

---

[1] Baker, C., (2018). Mental health statistics for England: prevalence, services and funding. [online] Available at: https://researchbriefings.parliament.uk/ResearchBriefing/Summary/SN06988 [Accessed 18 Mar. 2019].

Health Organization, in 2017, "Globally, more than 300 million people suffer from depression, the leading cause of disability." and "More than 260 million are living with anxiety disorders."[2]

Some questions I like to see answered when I study different therapy models are:

- What they were based on when they were created;

- What kind of issues each of them can be good for;

- If they actually do work or are nothing but a scam;

- What constitutes a good therapist of that specific practice;

- What kind of approach does each take;

- And what are some of the most common

---

[2] (2017). WHO | World Mental Health Day 2017. [online] Available at: https://www.who.int/mental_health/world-mental-health-day/2017/en/ [Accessed 18 Mar. 2019].

techniques.

In this ebook, I will be answering these and other questions, using hypothetical practical examples of situations to make it easier for the reader to understand, about two specific forms of psychotherapy: Cognitive Behavioral Therapy and Neuro-Linguistic Programming. The first one is a talking therapy that gives the client tools to consciously identify and correct dysfunctional thinking patterns; while the second one works at a deeper level, reaching a person's subconscious and their internal representations of the world and implementing techniques to be more positive and successful in that part of the brain.

If this ebook sparked an interest in you, you might have already heard of CBT and/or of NLP. Perhaps you have not, but you are considering enrolling in some type of therapy. Or maybe you are just curious. Whichever one you are, this ebook is indeed going to be helpful for you. The goal is for you to end it with a better notion of what constitutes each of the practices and with more knowledge that you can take into consideration when it is time to decide if you finish the book with a decision made, even better!

So, to help you, I will be talking about CBT and NLP alternatively throughout the book, in a Compare and Contrast kind of style, and in the end I will make a summary of the main differences and the main similarities between the two, followed by a series of questions that might steer you into a certain direction instead of the other.

Now, onto chapter 1, where I will let you know the definition of each of the practices, as well as their origins!

Chapter 1: Definitions

What is Cognitive Behavioral Therapy (CBT)?

If you look up the official definition of Cognitive Behavioral Therapy, you will find numerous results. Of course, they all convey the same idea, but for the purpose of this ebook, I will take the definition I find to be the clearest, in case some of the readers are not familiar with this type of therapy. According to the National Alliance on Mental Illness (NAMI), CBT "focuses on exploring relationships among a person's thoughts, feelings, and behaviors. During CBT, a therapist will actively work with a person to uncover unhealthy patterns of thought and how they may be causing self-destructive behaviors and beliefs."[3] So, the main idea when it comes to CBT is to change an individual's dysfunctional

---

[3] (n.d.). Psychotherapy | NAMI: National Alliance on Mental Health. [online] Available at: https://www.nami.org/learn-more/treatment/psychotherapy [Accessed 18 Mar. 2019].

thinking patterns and, by doing so, allow them to free themselves from any psychological conditions they might be suffering from.

Moreover, if you break down the name of the therapy, you easily understand its components and what it is based on:

Cognitive: from the Latin "cognoscere", which means "to know". It refers to an individual's conscious mental processes of "acquisition, storage, manipulation, and retrieval of information"[4]. In other words, it refers to what we daily and continuously do with the billions of nerve cells in our brains: every time we learn something new, every time we process information, react to information and use information that we previously stored to make decisions. You used your cognition to learn how to write and read, to memorize a part of the

---

[4] (2015). What Is Cognition & Cognitive Behaviour - Cambridge Cognition | Cambridge Cognition. [online] Available at: https://www.cambridgecognition.com/blog/entry/what-is-cognition [Accessed 18 Mar. 2019].

information you've been exposed to in your life (and forget the other part), to make decisions from "What am I going to have for lunch today?" to "What do I want to study in university?", to associate a certain smell with a memory, to make a plan and achieve a goal, and so many more mental processes.

Behavioral: it refers to an individual's reactions to what is happening around him or her. This can be a facial expression, a movement, a verbal response and so on. If someone says a funny joke, you laugh. If you feel hungry, you eat something. If you don't like speaking in public, you might get so nervous that you miss opportunities in your career and... I could go on forever, but I think you get the idea.

So how does CBT combine these two elements and use them to the advantage of people with a given psychological issue? Well, the logic is that the cognitive defines the behavioral. If your cognition is telling you that a certain event is negative, it will reflect on the way you react and the way you behave. Even if your brain is playing tricks on you and there is nothing inherently negative connected with that event. And how do we fix this? We challenge those unfavorable thoughts and emotions. We take on a solution-oriented approach, where the main goal is to tackle a specific problem and solve it in a short period of time (usually in 5 to 10 months, which makes this kind of therapy quite cost-effective), by identifying the harmful thinking patterns, working on them through countless techniques (I will give you some examples of these in Chapter 2) and, finally, breaking the cycle of destructive behaviors that was happening. And that is what Cognitive Behavioral Therapy exercises and practices are based on.

Notice the focus with CBT is not on actual events, but on the feelings and thoughts that those events trigger - that is one of the characteristics that sets Cognitive Behavioral Therapy apart from other types of psychotherapy. The therapist will also not pay particular attention to the person's past, but to the present issue that the individual is struggling with and how to make things better for the future. So if you take one of the examples mentioned before: let's say a person goes to a CBT therapist because of their issues about public speaking. Their sessions will not be conducted in a way that tries to figure out what happened in the person's past that causes them to now have major symptoms of anxiety when in a situation where they have to talk in front of several people. Instead, the therapist will explain what anxiety is and, in teamwork with the client and with a lot of homework, they will establish efficient ways of turning that anxiety into a positive feeling that leads to positive behaviors. The homework is essential, since the person will not only have to gain the ability to actually use the exercises in moments of anxiety but also because eventually the therapy sessions will come to an end and the coping strategies learned should be taken and applied for life, even when the individual is not undertaking psychological support anymore. And all of that comes with practice!

What Is the Origin of CBT?

Although it has gained more popularity in the last decade or so, the foundation of Cognitive Behavioral Therapy is not recent. The basis of CBT can be traced back to the later 40s, early 50s, when the American psychologist B. F. Skinner and the South African psychiatrist Joseph Wolpe introduced the concept of behavioral therapy; the "official" birth of CBT goes back to the 1960s and the credit is usually shared between the American psychologist Albert Ellis and the also American psychiatrist Aaron Beck.

The ABC Model

In 1957, Albert Ellis came up with the concept of basic irrational assumptions, i.e., things people believe that in reality are not true and that end up messing with their happiness and quality of life; and with the ABC Model, that would, years after, be very relevant to the establishment of CBT by

Aaron Beck. The ABC Model is a relationship between three elements:

- **Activating Event**: something that happens and causes a high emotional response.

- **Belief**: harmful thoughts that resulted from the Activating Event, often the reason why we believe it occurred.

- **Consequence**: emotions and actions that the Belief triggers.

According to Ellis, the Activating Event doesn't cause the Consequence directly. Instead, it is how the person interprets the event that leads them to feel or act a certain way. This is easy to understand if we think about our fears and our friends' fears. For instance, I am extremely scared of the ocean. It makes me feel nervous to the point where I don't go to the beach anymore. The other day, I was talking to a friend about it and he feels the exact opposite: he loves the ocean and going to the beach is one of his favorite things to do during Summer. See how the exact same situation creates two completely different emotions? It is because at some point I acquired the Belief that if I go in the ocean, I won't be strong enough and I will end up drowning; while he sees it as a fun adventure.

As a solution to the ABC Model, in 1955, Ellis came up with Rational Emotive Behavior Therapy (REBT), with the foundation that a lot of people do not realize that many of their negative thoughts are irrational. We don't allow ourselves to feel as good as we could, and that is not only very energy consuming (particularly emotionally), but also leads us to make decisions that are not the best for ourselves and/or for those around us. REBT is now considered a type of CBT and also has the goal of identifying the client's negative thinking cycles and change them into positive ones. REBT can be very useful to minimize feelings of guilt, procrastination, extreme anger with no reason and unhealthy habits, and it teaches the clients the concept of Unconditional Self Acceptance (USA), that is, the concept of detaching yourself from what you do and the way you are, accepting the fact that you are a human being, and human beings make mistakes. You don't think you are the best person when you do something good, but you also don't martyrize yourself when you make a mistake - you accept both kinds of situations and look at them as learning opportunities. It's a very peaceful type of therapy that provides the person with a better liking for taking risks and opens up doors in life that they did not even know existed before.

The Cognitive Triad

A decade after, in 1967, Aaron Beck takes inspiration on Ellis' ABC Model and creates the Cognitive Triad or Negative Triad, that explains an individual's thinking processes when they are suffering from depression. Again, the model is based on three elements, but this time these elements are three kinds of negatives thoughts: of the self, of the world, and of the future. These are backed by the Cognitive Bias and the Negative Self-Schemas, two concepts also defined by Beck.

The Negative Self-Schemas are a set of negative thoughts and beliefs that the person has about themselves, that result from a group of memories of the person's life. The Cognitive Bias is a set of mental distortions that describe the way people who suffer from depression distort information; for example, thinking that everything in their life is going wrong when one single bad thing happens. There are at least 45 Cognitive Biases, but talking about every single one them would be too exhausting for you as a reader and would make this ebook excessively long, so I will only mention 5 of the most typical ones:

- **Bandwagon Effect:** if you are on the Internet, I am sure you have been aware of the trends that come and go over time. Who doesn't remember the Mannequin Challenge from a little over two years ago, for example? It was a huge phenomenon of the online world - I remember even my family and I did it on the Christmas' Eve of that year. But why? Simply because everyone else was doing it and, for some reason, we wanted to be a part of it. And we didn't even post it online! Some other examples of the Bandwagon examples are the fashion trends people adopt, moving to a certain country or city because it is the new hot place where everyone is going or even voting for a certain candidate in the elections, purely because you have a feeling they are going to be the winner. So, you guessed it, the Bandwagon Effect happens when someone does something solely because everyone else is doing it and it happens because, as human beings, we are very easily influenced and we do not like feeling like we are not a part of something or like it is us against the world. Now, things like fashion and moving are quite innocent examples of this effect, but it can also lead to more harmful situations. One example was the extremely dangerous game of the Blue Whale Challenge, that was so popular between teens in 2016 (to the point where you probably heard about it in the news back then) and where they were challenged to do things like self-harm and, ultimately, kill themselves.

- **Gambler's Fallacy:** if you have ever played Rock, Paper, Scissors, you have probably used the Gambler's Fallacy as a way to decide which one of the three you were going to choose. Oftentimes, we base our choice on what our opponent chose on the previous round. If they chose Scissors, in our mind the chances of them playing Scissors again are lower, so we feel safer playing Scissors on the next round. But the truth is there is always a 33,3333% chance that they will play Scissors (just like there is always the same chance that they will play Rock or Paper). That is what the

Gambler's Fallacy consists of: we let ourselves believe that previous results of a situation that is 100% random (such as gambling) have an impact on future results. The name of this Cognitive Bias was inspired by something that happened back in 1913, when something that had a very, very low probability of happening (1 in 136823184, to be specific) happened: they landed in the color black 29 times in a row, at a roulette wheel. Believing in the Gambler's Fallacy can put someone in dangerous situations, when they believe something will always go well, based on the fact that up until now they were lucky enough for it to go well, so they don't even consider the fact that that might change anytime.

- **Von Restorff Effect:** a theory introduced in the early thirties by the German psychiatrist Hedwig von Restorff (hence the name), after a study on memory that he conducted. This effect, that is also referred to as the Isolation Effect, is based on the idea that in a group of multiple similar things, the one that is different stands out and is more likely to be remembered. It is based on this effect that when we wrote essays in college, we would make the most important sentences bold or that when we were studying, we would highlight the most important parts. Those games where you see a square full of Ms and somewhere in the middle there is an N that you have to find is a test to the Von Restorff Effect, for example. If you saw an N by itself you would not pay particular attention to it, but amidst the Ms, it stands out to you. This concept is widely used by designers and advertisers, because it is very useful to direct the customer to the most important part of the piece: to the CTA, for instance.

- **Placebo Effect**: when I was a kid, I used

to get motion sickness all the time and so my parents started giving me this pink liquid (that, to my defence, truly looked like real medicine) every time we had to go somewhere by car. Years went by, I grew up, my "severe" motion sickness disappeared and life went on. A couple of years ago, my parents confessed to me that that magical liquid was not for motion sickness, it was simply a vitamin supplement. But then... how did it make my nausea go away every single time? Well, the answer is this fourth cognitive bias: the Placebo Effect. The word "Placebo" comes from Latin and it means "I will please". "Placebo Effect" is a term that is commonly used in the world of medicine, defined as a beneficial effect that resulted from the administration of a certain drug or treatment, but that cannot be credited to the properties of this drug or treatment, since there is no active substance in them that could treat the condition. The benefits happen purely because the patient believes it will (which just comes to show how powerful your our brains truly are!). It might sound somewhat irresponsible and unethical and you might feel as if someone is tricking you (which, deep down, they are), but doctors have been prescribing placebos for a long time, in cases where it is safe, when the patient can't take the medications they would suggest (because of an allergy to one of the components, for instance) or when there is no other solution to the problem. So a lot of times, they end up prescribing vitamins, just like my dear father and mother did with me years ago, because they will not cause any harm and will still make the patient feel like they are taking medicine and curing their sickness. but the point here is: the Placebo Effect is all a product of your brain and that is why it constitutes as a Cognitive Bias.

- **Stereotyping:** this is a touchy one, because no one likes to admit that they sometimes stereotype people. However, it is natural for us to do it. As human beings, we like to put (and be put) in boxes and for each box, we associate a set of characteristics. We associate genders, skin colors, nationalities, sexual orientations and many other groups of labels with certain qualities and capabilities. This can be seen as a way of organizing people and making life as a community smoother, but it is crucial to know that not everyone in a certain box has all the characteristics associated with it. Stereotyping becomes damaging and even dangerous when we are talking about people who cannot internalize that although stereotypes are natural to come to mind, we are all human beings, so we are all the same, but different. That is the case, for example, of people who still, to this day, believe that women have fewer capabilities and that they are not as smart as men, and for that reason if someone of the male gender and someone of the female gender have the exact same position in the company, the first one often has a higher salary. For some reason, throughout history, women were constantly portrayed as less than men, particularly when it comes to their intellect, to the point that "like a girl" is often used as an offense. However, if we stop to think about it rationally and as I said before, we easily realize (or should realize, at least) that men and women are all human beings. So we need to question ourselves (and others): how can a gender tell so much about an individual's ability to do a job well? It is important to not let stereotypes condition other people's lives and take away from them rights that they should always have, which is something that, unfortunately, happens quite regularly with minorities.

It was as a solution to this Cognitive Triad that Beck created CBT. Although it was very similar to REBT, there were some aspects of Ellis' therapy that didn't make sense to Beck, hence the need to create a new and improved version of it. For example, to Ellis, the therapy was all about teaching and learning. The therapist was a teacher. This meant that there was no need for a good relationship between therapist and client - as long as knowledge was passed on, the goal was accomplished. Beck didn't agree with this mindset. To him, it is crucial that the therapist and the client have a good relationship since CBT is so much about the collaboration and teamwork between the two parties. Another aspect that sets the two types of therapy apart is how much of the work is put on the client. Ellis would go for a more confrontational approach; while for Beck, it made sense that the clients got to the conclusions by themselves (with support and guidance of a professional, of course), which is evident by how much input is needed for this kind of therapy.

In a nutshell, Beck looked at the model Ellis had created and gave it a more emotional-oriented approach. And like that, Cognitive Behavioral Therapy was born.

What Is Neuro-Linguistic Programming (NLP)?

Neuro-Linguistic Programming seems like a rather complicated name, and if you look up the definition online, you will most likely not find that much conclusive information since there is not one widely accepted definition yet, but the main idea of the practice is not hard to understand. NLP is based on the relationship between our conscious mind and our unconscious mind and, according to this practice, we get information and process it using our five senses, which is how our perception of the world is formed; in other words, each of us has our own definition of reality, that is a result of how we perceive the world. This means that the world and the situations themselves don't matter: what matters is how those situations make you feel (hence the fact that the exact same situation can originate two opposite feelings and reactions in two different people). When you decide to do an NLP training, what you get in the end is an instruction manual for your own brain. The big objective on NLP is to teach people how to communicate with themselves (as well as with others) and put their conscious and unconscious minds in sync, in order to, in due time, pinpoint successful patterns of behavior that can be recreated to achieve their goals with greater ease and efficiency.

Following the same logic as I did with CBT, I will divide the name and explain each part, so that it is easier to understand what NLP is all about. Each of these three words refers to one of the three components that play a part in NLP: the mind, the language, and the behavior.

Neuro: represents the mind. Every single day, we are bombarded with gigantic amounts of information. From interactions with other people, to things we read online or in books, to programs we watch on TV, to the millions of ads distributed all over and so much more. Obviously none of us retains 100% of this information; we can all process the exact same information in completely different ways through our five senses and the influence that this information has on our bodies varies from person to person, and it is the "neuro" that is responsible for this division between what we forget and what (and how) we process and retain. This component constitutes the most basic mental map there is - sometimes referred to as "First Access" - that is composed by what John Grinder (I will talk about him soon) called VAKOG: Visual, Auditory, Kinaesthetic (meaning sensory), Olfactory and Gustatory.

Linguistic: represents the language. If in the first stage we receive the information through the neuro, the next step is the responsibility of the linguistic component. What happens here is that we take the information our brain chose to process and we give it our own meaning, by accrediting language to what we get through each of our senses. This is where the unconscious becomes conscious and where the second mental map, called Linguistic Map (or Linguistic Representation), comes in.

Programming: represents the behavior. It is the result of the combination of the Neuro and the Linguistic, that stems in certain actions and reactions. In NLP, this component refers to the use of tools to recode how an individual perceives some things, specifically the negative ones, and to shift their (negative) behaviors that result from that perception into more positive, productive ones, which are the two ultimate objectives of an NLP treatment.

So the logic behind NLP is that, in order to recode the way our brain responds to a certain situation (Programming), we need to change the way the brain works and processes the information (Neuro), through the use of language (Linguistic).

What Is the Origin of NLP?

Remember before, when I told you I would talk about John Grinder? Well, this is where he comes in. The concept of Neuro-Linguistic Programming goes back to the 1970s and it was developed by two men: Dr. Richard Bandler and John Grinder.

Dr. Richard Bandler is an American mathematician, author and self-help trainer, who has written and co-written countless books about psychology, communication, and how to reprogramme one's brain and who has also created other practices, namely the Design Human Engineering (DHE) and the Neuro Hypnotic Repatterning (NHR). Bandler was the first one to introduce the idea of NLP, defining it as "A model of interpersonal communication chiefly concerned with the relationship between successful patterns of behaviour and the subjective experiences underlying them", as well as "A system of alternative therapy based on this which seeks to educate people in self-awareness and effective communication, and to change their patterns of mental and emotional behaviour"[5].

In the early seventies, when Bandler started working on what would become NLP, he was doing it with one of his good friends, Frank Pucelik, who was also studying at the University of California Santa Cruz and who is now a personal coach, consultant and author (in some versions of the story, a number of other students are also said to have been a part of this group, but it is not known what is actually the truth). At this point, their goal was to create a Gestalt therapy 2.0., that they could apply in their own lives: Pucelik wanted to find a way of dealing with his PTSC caused by his traumatic past in Vietnam and Bandler had more academic reasons, since he was, at the time, editing Fritz Perls' work named "The Gestalt Approach and Eyewitness to

---

[5] (n.d.). What is NLP? | Neuro-Linguistic Programming | Influencing brain behaviour through use of language | NLP Life Training. [online] Available at:
http://www.nlplifetraining.com/what-is-nlp/index.html
[Accessed 18 Mar. 2019].

Therapy". For better context, the Gestalt therapy was a holistic practice developed by the German psychiatrist and psychotherapist Fritz Perls, that was built on the idea that a person is the "totality of mind, body, emotions and spirit who experiences reality in a way unique to themselves" (which makes sense when you learn the fact that "Gestalt" is the German word for "whole").

The two students would get together 2 to 3 times each week and at one point, John Grinder - who is currently a linguistic, author and speaker born in January of 1940 in the United States, and was Bandler and Pucelik's professor at the time - joined the two students in their meetings, where they would not only discuss the Gestalt therapy, but any other concepts introduced and habits adopted by people that they considered to be great communicators in several different industries. At first, Grinder did not do much except observing and listening but, eventually, he started giving his input as well, to the point where he is now considered the main character in the history of NLP. He was the piece that was missing to the puzzle since the two students were doing a good job reaching very interesting conclusions, but they were not quite sure how to share those conclusions with others and use them to improve other people's quality of life. Well, Grinder was a Linguistics professor, so he was the perfect person to help them with the communication component.

The 6 Pillars of NLP

Bandler, Grinder, and Pucelik came up with the 4 pillars of NLP. These four elements constitute the foundation of NLP and they are what someone undergoing an NLP treatment or training should keep in mind to achieve their goals and to be (more) successful. When worked on simultaneously and brought to their full potential, these 4 pillars can be the solution to those looking for more success in their career or better well-being in terms of mental health.

Outcome Thinking

Outcome Thinking is related to a person's goals. It is about knowing what you want and what you don't want in your life before you start working for it. When you are able to imagine the future and what you want it to be like for yourself, it becomes easier for you to draw a plan and make decisions regarding which steps you need to take towards achieving it. Of course, in some situations, making the final decision about what you want is very difficult - after all, who hasn't felt indecisive before? - but that is exactly what Neuro-Linguistic Programming can help you learn: the skills to effectively assess the pros and cons of each decision and ultimately reach a profitable conclusion.

Having a grasp of your Outcome Thinking is the first step towards increasing your success and productivity, kind of like what the Fundamental Law of Attraction claims, and it does not matter how big or small your goal is, the focus is still the same: the fact that you clearly know what you want is a big step towards achievement.

For NLP, the core ideals when it comes to Outcome Thinking is that you should always think of your goals with a positive point of view ("I can do it" instead of "I wish I could do it") and that they should be SMART:

- **Specific:** as I have said in the last paragraph - it is crucial that you have a clear idea of your goal. think about it this way: between the goals "I want to be more active" and "I want to learn how to surf", which ones sounds easier to plan?

- **Measurable:** you will want to know how successful you were and that is only possible for measurable objectives.

- **Achievable:** it is great to be determined and to want more, but setting a goal that you know you can't achieve, at least at that point in your life, is a recipe for failure. Setting the goal of "I want to learn how to surf" when you don't know how to swim is an example of an unachievable goal; the first goal should be "I want to learn how to swim". Sometimes it is all about taking baby steps and not going straight to the biggest goal of them all!

- **Realistic:** that is, on the same level as your circumstances. If you set your goals way too high and know that you don't have the resources to achieve them, it just becomes unrealistic and it can even make you lose your motivation.

- **Time-bound:** when you put a deadline on your goal, it is easier for you to organize your plan and measure results. It also puts a healthy amount of pressure on you to keep working (emphasis on the words "healthy amount". Don't put so much pressure that it makes you feel nothing but stressed out until you reach your goal).

Sensory Acuity

Sensory Acuity, also known as Sensory Awareness, consists of the way each individual sees and perceives the world through their senses of olfact, sight, touch, taste and smell, which allows them to understand what is happening around them. It is what we use when building rapport with someone else, it greatly affects our Outcome Thinking and it says a lot about how we can effectively communicate with others and how others can effectively communicate with us.

Some people notice a lot of what happens around, as well as within them and tend to memorize a lot of details, while others are not as observant. For NLP, this is important because those who notice more details, generally have a better understanding of how close or far they are to achieving the goals they set and they are also more aware of how another person responds to different kinds of communication, therefore being able to adapt in an easier manner. Besides that, having a sharp Sensory Awareness also helps in the sense that the person can think of a bigger plethora of paths they can take to achieve their goals, which is very helpful for the fourth pillar in the list, Behavioral Flexibility, but we will get there. So, those of us who are more distracted and don't take in as many details can recur to NLP to master their observation and attention skills.

Behavioral Flexibility

Even when you know which goals you want to achieve and when you have become a more detail-oriented person, your plan might still not work. We have all failed before and, in some situations, simply given up because of that. Behavioral Flexibility refers to the person's ability to adapt when a certain situation does not have the outcome they first imagined. Remember in the last paragraph, when I said that having a good Sensory Awareness can be advantageous for the Behavioral Flexibility? Well, that is because the fourth pillar is all about a person's ability to say "OK, this is not working" and then have the flexibility to choose another option that their sensory awareness allowed them to come up with and adopt it in order to, in the end, still achieve success.

That kind of mindset is something that most people still need to work on. I mean, it is so much easier to give up! NLP claims that a bigger Behavioral Flexibility is often the synonym of more success. With NLP, the person learns how to not let failures bring them down and how to see them as a healthy challenge and an opportunity to learn. NLP uses Robert Dilts' six hierarchical neurological levels - six groups of factors that have an impact on the person's life (and that affect the levels below and may affect the levels above) - to itemize what a person can question and where they can make changes. I will talk a little bit about each of those levels and mention the ways someone can change them, when faced with a specific problem - let's say we are talking about Catherine and she is struggling at home, where she cannot seem to make her parents understand that it will make her happier to pursue a career in music, instead of law, as they had always planned for her. The whole situation is making her very anxious about her future, since she still wants to please her parents, and that causes her to seem a little bit uncertain about her love and desire to be a musician.

- **Environment:** the circumstances in which a particular situation happens. Catherine could change the environment by talking to one parent at a time, so that they don't have the other one to support them. This approach might make it easier to make them understand, since there will probably not be as much resistance on their end.

- **Behavior:** the "what" and "how" of the action. Catherine could change her behavior by adopting a more assertive posture and having a more confident discourse when speaking to her parents.

- **Capability:** the way the person does things. Catherine could change her capability by working on her communication skills with her parents.

- **Beliefs:** what matters to the person, as well as their expectations. Catherine could change her beliefs by assessing the why of her choice of music over law school, and then interiorizing that she is her own person and that she cannot give so much importance to what her parents expect of her, to the point that it causes her anxiety about following her own dreams.

- **Identity:** the person's sense of self. She could change this by working on her sense of self-worth, by seeing herself as a go-getter who will be successful as a musician and prove to her parents that that is what she was born to do, and by putting her dreams first.

- **Spirituality:** a person's purpose in life.

Catherine can tackle this last level by understanding if she will bring more to the world as a musician or as a lawyer, which one she believes deep inside her that she was born to be and if she is motivated enough to follow her dream even without the support of her parents.

Rapport

The Rapport relates to the quality of a person's relationships, both with others and with the self and it is crucial for all stages: establishing goals, being aware of what happens and changing plans when needed. For building and caring for these relationships, the person needs to have a rapport established. To do this, the individual should be able to recognize the fact that everyone sees and perceives the world in a different way and that, for them to have a connection with person X, they have to be willing to meet them halfway, between both of the perceptions.

The word "rapport" originates from the French

language, in which it means harmony and agreement, between others. So in other words, it refers to the tools a person needs to be in harmony with those around them, as well as with themselves.

Chances are you have a good Rapport with a number of people. You have good relationships even with people who have lifestyles, communication styles, personalities and even ideals that you do not exactly identify with. Sometimes it is natural, you get a little bit out of your comfort zone, the other person does the same, and when you realize, you are both on the same level and wave. You both adapt your posture, your tone, your language and suddenly you are acquaintances and then friends! I mean, don't you have that one friend that always makes you think "Wow, I never thought I would be friends with someone like this?" but who you still love unconditionally? Or haven't you been to a store where you usually wouldn't go - and where you don't seem to fit in at all - but ended up really enjoying the environment and staff there? Sometimes it is even easier and you and the person have a lot in common and don't need to adjust that much.

However, meeting people who are different than you, which is bound to happen during your journey to achieve your goals, may not always be that easy. NLP can give you the skills to find and give comfort when you meet others, building a Rapport and finding harmony even when the differences seem way too big to maintain a connection, instead of looking at those differences as an obstacle. The fundamental way NLP allows you to do this is by helping you focus on what you have in common with other people, instead of what you don't. Learning this skill means learning how to make everyone around you feel comfortable and accepted, how to be a good leader that truly cares about those you lead, as well as those you provide services for; and how to be overall more open to learning about things that are completely foreign to you.

Besides these 4 pillars, there is another one that is not as talked about as much, yet it is just as important for this practice: the Presuppositions.

NLP Presuppositions

There are 14 NLP presuppositions (in some sources you will find more than 14, but for this e-book I will only talk about those), i.e. 14 ideas that summarize what the NLP mindset is all about and explain the philosophy behind the practice (which is why you will find some points that I already covered above). They work as the bible of NLP and the person who is undergoing NLP therapy sees them as the truth and as a guide for their life. These presuppositions are:

- **Respect the world model of those around you.**

You should never assume that your map of reality is right, and everyone else who sees things differently is wrong. According to NLP, you should accept the fact that everyone perceives the world differently, therefore you should be able to respect other people's world models.

- **The meaning of your communication is determined by the response you get.**

Your communication is more than what you say or do (or want to say or do). When a person doesn't understand what you intend to share with them, that says something about your ability to communicate, whether it is verbally or nonverbally. Moreover, if whatever you are trying to convey doesn't reach the other end, it means that you are not communicating properly and you might need to work on those skills.

- **A person is not their behavior.**

Particularly, their unsuccessful behavior. In other words, a person is more than their mistakes. It is important that one is capable of seeing their flaws and mistakes as things that can be fixed, rather than as something that defines them and that will forever be a part of who they are and the reason why they will never succeed. This applies to one's view of themselves, but also of others.

When people around you make what is considered to be a mistake, you should not judge them. You should accept them and help them change that particular behavior.

- **People make the best choice they can in their circumstances.**

When someone makes a decision, it is in their mind, the best decision they could make according to their map of reality at that moment; even if others see it as a harmful decision that will not lead them to the desired outcome. No one decides something with the mindset of "I will choose this because it will fail". So, even if in the end it does not work, the choice that was made was the best one for that specific person in those specific circumstances.

- **The map is not the territory.**

What we think and feel is not the absolute truth. Our map of reality - i.e., the way we see and interpret the world and the way that makes us act and react - changes over time. You can challenge your maps, change them, improve them and expand them. No one's world map is static because life teaches us lessons and we learn with each decision we make.

- **There is no failure, only feedback.**

We all make decisions that end up not working and a lot of times we see that as a failure. For NLP Practitioners, there is no such thing as failure. Every decision you make has a result and from that, you can either discover that that was the right way to go in order to achieve that goal, or the exact opposite: that next time you should not do it that way and that you can do this or that in a different manner. Either way, you always learn something, you always get feedback. Seeing it as such is a matter of keeping a positive attitude.

- **We all have the resources we need to achieve our goals (or, if we don't, we can create them).**

According to this presupposition, we all have

what we need within ourselves. We might just need to work in order to find those resources. If someone lives in a pessimistic state of mind, there is no use to all the resources they have in them, because it is not possible for the individual to reach them. He or she is not even conscious of them! When this person, however, changes their mindset and behavior to a more positive one, they start seeing the power they have within themselves and that is an extremely strong tool to accomplish the set goals.

- **Every behavior has a positive intention.**

Every action we take has a positive purpose; the thing is that it can be positive for others or for the self. In a summarized way, when we do something altruistic, the intention is positive for others and when we do something egoistic, the intention is positive for ourselves. Either way, there is always someone who is supposed to benefit from the behavior.

- **All procedures should increase wholeness.**

The decisions we make and actions we take should have wholeness as one of their goals, because it is very easy and very common for us to fragment our behaviors and become a different person in different contexts, in such as way that makes it difficult to be consistent in our communication and to stay true to who we really are and what we really believe in.

- **Everyone has the ability to control their minds and, therefore, their results.**

This one is very connected to number 7, that states that everyone has the resources they need. We have all heard about the power of the mind and how we can be in charge of it. Using your mind to its full potential is not easy and that is not what NLP says; however, it does say that you have a choice of either being defeated by a certain kind of feedback (remember, there are no failures!) or having a positive mindset. And of course, that will have an effect on your future results. I think by now you can figure out which option leads to better outcomes!

- **The most important information about a person is their behavior.**

Now I know that this might seem a little bit contradictory of number 3, but it is not and I will explain why. What this presupposition means is that, although a person is not their behaviors, these behaviors do say something about them. It is impossible for you to know what goes through people's minds, so if you did not calibrate on their behaviors, you would not be able to get any information about them.

- **The more Behavior Flexibility you have, the more you can control the system.**

The more ability to adapt and change plans you have, the bigger competitive advantage you have compared to others with a smaller Behavior

Flexibility. Who would you bet is more likely to get to the finish line: someone with a plan A or someone with a plan A, a plan B and a plan C? The more options of paths to achieve the outcome you have, the bigger your chances of success are.

- **The mind and the body are a system and they affect each other.**

We all feel this connection all the time in different levels and either in a negative or a positive manner. We know that the mind influences the body: stress can cause headaches; panic attacks can cause nausea; happiness can prevent sickness; self-empowerment can help with weight loss. And that it also works the other way around, when the body influences the mind: someone who has a severe physical illness may get depressed because of their situation; when a person achieves their ideal weight and body shape they may become more confident; when you exercise, your endorphins make you feel happier. The mind-and-body system should always be taken into account when treating both physical and psychological issues.

- **Choice is better than no choice.**

Having a choice means you get to be in control. As presupposition number 12 mentions, having options is a great sign! Would you be more excited about going into a restaurant with 10 options on their menu or a restaurant that only served one meal? When you have a choice, you are the one controlling your destiny and you have the opportunity to draw your own journey, learn with the missteps and to be responsible for your desired outcomes. Only having one option means not being able to choose and ultimately, having to settle. Settling is never the goal!

The NLP Communication Model

In 1988, over one decade after Bandler, Grinder, and Pucelik introduced the concept of Neuro-Linguistic Programming, the NLP Communication Model was created by two men - Tad James, an American Personal Success Coach,

NLP Master Trainer, and author, and Wyatt Woodsmall, an also American Master Trainer, internationally recognized NLP expert and author - and it became a component of extreme importance for the understanding and practice of NLP.

This model explains how the human brain processes information, which factors play a part in the procedure and what aftermath that has in our state, behavior, and physiology. By doing so, it becomes a very useful model to explain how we build our maps of reality and how we can make amendments when that is necessary. It works on the basis that all the information we take in, we take in unconsciously. Considering that we receive about 4 million impulses every single second, just imagine if you had to consciously choose which information is relevant and you will keep and which is unnecessary and you will choose to ignore... you would not do anything else in your life!

There are three fundamental components to the

NLP Communication Model: the sensory channels, the filters, and the processes, that play a part in the model at different stages.

Stage 1: The external stimuli

Firstly, the external information gets to the individual through their sensory channels, that is their five senses (also known as VAKOG), so:

- Visual: what you see.

- Auditory: what you hear.

- Kinesthetic: what you feel (both physically and emotionally).

- Olfactory: what you smell.

- Gustatory: what you taste.

Stage 2: The filtering process

The filters are the things an individual runs the stimulus they get through the VAKOG by, that will (unconsciously) help them decide what they will do with that information and how they will react to it. There are 6 filters:

- **Meta-Programs**

A person's Meta-Program is their first mental process, it consists of the way they handle information and some consider that it is something we are all born with. They are strongly connected to a person's personality and they are continuously developed by other mental filters in this list, such as the Memories and the Values. Meta-Programs are important in NLP because they help us have an idea of a person's state, and behaviors; and they can also be changed internally - in other words, they're a great aid to communicating effectively. Here is a practical example: let's say Maggie is at work and her boss decides to give her a bigger challenge than she has ever had to deal with in her position, up until that point. Maggie's Meta-Programs, however, are set to make her believe that she is not capable of successfully taking on said challenge, because at her previous job, she used to feel overwhelmed often. Due to that, Maggie assumes that what happened once will happen every time - she generalizes - and that makes her lose an opportunity to advance in her career.

- **Decisions**

Everytime a human being makes a decision, they learn something and that affects the way they perceive the world. This can be useful, in the sense that you don't have to learn the same thing over and over again. But it can also be limiting, if you lose the ability of challenging what you have learned from previous decisions. For instance, Courtney is a comedian. She performs at a small bar and, one day, she is invited to play for a much bigger audience and, although, she knows she will not have time to prepare a show that will make her proud, she still says yes. The night of the performance comes and she is not happy with how the show went down. In future situations, Courtney can either generalize and assume she was not born to perform for big audiences, or she can figure out what she did wrong and change it when the next opportunity arises. NLP's goal would be to train Courtney to go for the latter.

- **Values**

The filter "Values" is very connected to a person's childhood, upbringing, culture, and life experience. They are the things that matter to you and what you consider to be right and wrong, and they play a huge role in the process of decision-making. They change from context to context; that is, an individual's values - and, consequently, the way they process information and behave - may change from situation to situation. For example, Frankie is against animal cruelty. He knows he would never harm a cat or a dog, but he still eats animal products. In this situation, Frankie's inconsistency in Values results in him ignoring one part of the issue of animal cruelty.

- **Beliefs**

The Beliefs are the generalizations we make about ourselves, those around us and particular events, that we believe to be true and that can limit us on the way we process information. They can be compared to Values, but in a more conscious level. Imagine, for instance, that John is romantically interested in Anna, but believes that she is way out of his league. One day, Anna asks John out. However, and as interested as he is in her, John is reluctant to accept, because he put it in his mind that she can't be serious about it. John's belief that Anna is too good for him caused him to misrepresent her invite.

- **Memories**

As life goes on, your experience grows and you keep certain information in your memory that affects the way you perceive the world and that you later use to make decisions. So, like the filter of Decisions, your memories might be a useful resource to guide your life, but they are not globally correct. Just because you remember one instance when things went a certain way, it doesn't mean that they will always go that way and it is crucial to keep that in mind, so that you don't generalize or misinterpret a stimulus.

- **Language**

Language refers to words, i.e. the code you use to refer to something, the words you use to represent your version of reality. The Language influences what we do with a stimuli, because what the concept XYZ means to you might be completely different than what it means to the person next to you; if you two have a discussion about XYZ, that difference will have an impact on the quality of the discussion and on its outcomes, so it is important that, before you discuss, you reach a meaning of XYZ that you can both agree on.

Through the examples, you have probably understood what might happen to the stimuli during the filtering process - one of three things:

- **Deletion**

It is when you selectively pay attention to certain details of a situation, and ignore the other ones. It happens naturally in everyone's daily life, it is necessary that we omit certain parts of our experiences, otherwise we would most likely go insane. You are never really aware of your breathing until someone mentions it, right? Or when you are sitting on the sofa and watching TV, you are not thinking about how the sofa feels on your body, until you start feeling uncomfortable, are you? That kind of details does not matter and ignoring them leaves space in your brain for more relevant information. Another proof of deletion is how different people have different recollections of the exact same event, which is something that happens all the time. Without the ability of deletion, there would be way too much information for us to process and use to our advantage.

But, it also happens that sometimes we tune out details that are actually important and that can have limiting effects on our actions, as well as make it harder for others to fully understand our communication. When you speak with general words and omit certain information, instead of specifying what you mean, ideas can get lost in translation.

- **Distortion**

It is when we misinterpret and misrepresent the input that has gotten to us. Mind you, this process can be of great utility: imagining yourself achieving your goals and living your dream life in the future is a distortion and it can help you construct a plan to turn that dream into reality; or picturing several different outcomes of a decision. In fact, the bigger the ability to distort, the more fertile your imagination is.

But it can also be limiting, particularly when your distortion of something turns it into a negative thing. When you see someone in a negative light with no real reason, for example, or when you see a complex task as a recipe for disaster instead of as a healthy challenge that will make you grow. Another way in which Distortion can be harmful is when we assume without evidence. Your mind - your imagination - leads you to construct your own meanings of things and these meanings will not always match those of the people around you. That can negatively impact your communication with them. One way of minimizing that impact is by asking "why" before you just jump to the assumptions.

- **Generalization**

It is when you take one single experience, and apply it to all experiences that seem to be similar. This is natural to the human being and it is how we learn things. We see them, we experience them, we find out how they go. And next time, when we are in that situation, we have a better idea of how it will probably happen and what we should do about it. The keyword here is "probably" because, in order to grow and learn even more, we need to be able to accept that there are no absolute truths, therefore we cannot generalize with 100% accuracy.

Now for some people, generalizing can be a way of feeling safer. However, accepting every single generalization you make will cause more harm than security: you risk being judgmental, not taking the next step in your career, relationships or life in general and not feeling as fulfilled as you could. To fight unnecessary and limiting generalizations and look at everything we learn - positive and negative - as something that can make us grow as people, it can be helpful to internalize the NLP presupposition that says that there is no such thing as failure, but feedback; as well as to practice imagining what would happen if that generalization turned out to not be totally accurate, how you could adapt and what you could gain.

Stage 3: the Internal Representation, the State, the Physiology and Behavior

The two previous stages result in our internal representations (commonly referred to as I/R), that appear to us as images, sounds and words in our mind, which affect our internal feeling state (that is, the way that the information makes us feel), which in turn is related to, influences and is influenced by our physiology (how our body reacts when we feel that way). That is why we all associate certain postures and gestures with particular states of mind: when we think of nervousness, we generally imagine someone hunching down, almost trying to hide; yet when we think of confidence, we imagine someone with the opposite posture with a straight spine and their shoulders back, for example.

In the end, this Internal Representation, State and Physiology process determines our behavior. Ultimately, this is the process that all NLP exercises and techniques, no matter what the end goal is, mean to improve.

Chapter 2: How To Practice

How To Practice CBT

With a Therapist

When it comes to Cognitive Behavioral Therapy, you can choose to be followed by a professional and have their support during a short period of time (usually up until 10 months), especially if you are looking to fix a complex issue and, of course, if you can afford it. The sessions can be done in person, online (which is called i-CBT and can be a great start for people with such severe mental conditions that they don't feel comfortable leaving their house) or even through a phone call, either individually or in a group, and they usually last 30 to 60 minutes.

What To Look For in a CBT Therapist

First of all, I should say that you and your therapist should click as individuals, regarding their skills and expertise as a professional and that, at this stage, you should not worry too much if you can't open up to this person as much as you think you should. If you two are indeed a good match, that openness will come with time. However, there are a few traits that this kind of therapists generally present and that you can try and look for when you first meet them:

- They don't pressure you into sharing any information you don't feel comfortable sharing.

- They are easy to approach and show honest concern about the patient's problems. Since not everyone who goes into the professional's office is 100% ready to commit to the treatment, it is crucial that the therapist has the warmth to make them realize that that office is a safe space and that they are there for support and guidance. The therapist should be able to make the person feel like there is someone giving them a hand, purely because they want to help them feel better, and that it will be worth it to open up.

- They have good communication skills. CBT is an educational, talking therapy so there is nothing more important than being able to convey the information effectively.

- They have a positive attitude! A person with a pessimistic attitude working in a practice where the main goal is to turn the negative into positive does not sound like it would work, now does it?

And, of course, look for a licensed therapist, preferably with previous experience in Cognitive Behavioral Therapy. The therapist will most likely give you the opportunity to ask them questions, so take that time to find out more about their success rate, how long they have been practicing CBT, what is their training and any other factors you find relevant to understand their legitimacy in CBT.

The way the sessions are led depends on the

therapist, the client and the problem to be solved, but the general structure would be:

The First Sessions

Let's say you decide to give CBT a try. Before your first session, you may have a phone call where some questions are asked, in order to assess your state at that point and to let you know what you need to bring to the session (like a list of the problems you want to cover, for example).

The main goal during your first sessions of CBT will be for the therapist to understand what is troubling you. I mentioned before that a good relationship between therapist and client was something that Aaron Beck, the father of CBT, considered to be very important, so the session will start with introductions and a light conversation, for you to get to know each other and to make you realize that you are in a safe place and you can open up. Chances are you feeling a bit nervous about your first time with CBT (as you would probably feel with any kind of therapy), and it will be in the interest of your therapist to calm down those nerves before you start speaking about what brings you there.

After that, you will dive into the deeper conversation of the session - what is called the Mental Health Assessment - where the therapist will ask you questions about yourself, your past, your issue and how you have tried dealing with it and fixing in the past, but don't worry: they will never force you to talk about anything you don't feel comfortable talking about. Some of these questions may be:

- Describe your problem(s). What are the symptoms that you feel? What goes through your mind?

- How does this affect your daily life?

- What triggers these negatives feelings?

- Have you tried any kind of therapy before? If so, how did those experiences go?

- How long do you usually feel the symptoms for? How intense are they?

- What do you usually do to try and calm down the symptoms (either positive or negative coping systems)?

- What are the circumstances in which this problem usually arises (i.e., location, time of the day, company, etc.)?

- Do you have any habits that are a risk for you or for those around you (like self-harm, for example)?

The therapist will also want to know why you chose to try CBT and the goals you want to achieve by the end of the treatment (don't worry if you don't have those goals established at this point, it is something you can work on with your therapist). Through this conversation, the therapist will figure out if CBT is the right kind of therapy for your situation and, in case it is, if they have the best experience and expertise to help you or if they know another therapist that would be a better fit. You will also understand if you feel comfortable with Cognitive Behavioral Therapy and with that specific professional.

Once the therapist has a good understanding of who you are and what brought you to their office, they can work on a treatment plan that they will share with you. This will probably not happen right on your first session, but expect the therapist to be open with you about what is going to happen during your time with them, how many times you will need to meet up with them, what will be the approach and what kind of work you will have to do at home (and expect to have homework right from the first session). They will explain why you feel the symptoms you feel and how you can learn how to live with them and turn your mindset into a positive one. They might also give you some resources for you to read at home. As I said before, CBT is a very educational kind of therapy so these sessions will almost be like classes. You will learn new ways of thinking and why they (hopefully) work for your problem.

The Following Sessions

Now that your plan is laid out, it is time to start the actual therapy, where you will have a more active role, while the counselor listens and coaches you. The following sessions will be all about applying the treatment and working side by side with your therapist to do so. In the first stage, you will focus on the negative thoughts and emotions you have, by defining what you feel and think in moments of struggle and the actions that stem from that state of mind. Your therapist will probably ask you to have a journal where you can write it all down and keep up with the progress from session to session. When you have this list of thoughts and emotions, you analyze each of them. With the help of your therapist, you will understand if these are realistic or not and if they are holding you back from reaching your full potential in your life. During this period, your homework may be more of observation and noting down of your emotions and actions.

These subsequent sessions will all have a similar outline and this is when the therapist will teach you relaxation strategies, ways of rationalizing your thoughts, problem-solving techniques, mindfulness, and countless exercises to break the cycle of irrational negative thinking patterns. They will continuously underline the importance of homework, that at this phase will be more practical, and on each session you will do the revision of last session's homework; keep in mind that you should go into Cognitive Behavioral Therapy with commitment and the willingness to put in effort into the work. Applying the techniques you learn on your day-to-day life may not be an easy task, which is why during these sessions, the therapist will be open to discussing with you the difficulties you find yourself faced with, as well as the progress you are making.

The Final Session

After a while (usually a couple of months), you will start seeing your problem as something you are able to control and so the regularity of sessions will decrease until your therapist decides that you are ready to keep applying what you learned without their support. The decrease of frequency is done so that you are not suddenly left to deal with everything by yourself, as that could be too much of a "shock", and this way, the therapist can make sure you are indeed ready to take that step. But as I mentioned before, the goal of CBT is to turn you into your own therapist and, at some point, the time for your last session will come. This will be a closure session, where you will evaluate the work done, the progress and how you feel about continuing the work on your own.

By Yourself
Not everyone can afford a therapist, not everyone feels ready to share their struggles with a complete stranger or has time to do so, and CBT therapists aren't everywhere. That does not mean that not everyone can turn to CBT in order to feel better. Through the use of online resources and self-help books, you can apply CBT techniques

and exercises to your life without the support of a professional. If you choose this route though, know that you will have to be even more committed to making the therapy work, since you will not have someone regularly reminding you of the importance of doing your homework and of continuous practice.

Nevertheless, self-directed CBT can be extremely effective, in particular for people with mild symptoms, and there are studies to prove it, like the ones Cambridge University conducted. Their objective was to understand if self-help interventions could be effective to manage symptoms of depression and, after analyzing the 34 studies, they found that self-help techniques do have the potential to be beneficial, especially CBT techniques. Note that I am not saying you can completely cure anxiety by yourself - the practice of CBT with the monitoring of a professional is still proved to be more effective - but you can minimize the symptoms.

Three tips for those trying Cognitive Behavioral

Therapy at home are to:

- Choose a book or online course that you identify with, that seems to be a good choice for your circumstances and that is trustworthy. Take your time to do some research and read reviews and experiences by other people, since this book will end up doing the role of your therapist, by guiding and coaching you through the process.

- Set up an agenda, just like a therapist would do for you. Add your sessions in your calendar and plan out what you will be working on each day. Maybe the book or website you choose to follow will even have a schedule already set up and all you have to do is fit it into your daily life!

- Remind yourself of the importance of continuous practice. There is a reason why I keep mentioning it throughout this ebook and it is because it's essential that you regularly train your mind to think positive instead of negative.

How To Practice NLP

With a Professional

Similarly to CBT, there are different ways a person can practice Neuro-Linguistic Programming, one of them being with a professional. As I will dive into in a couple of chapters, NLP is generally used for two types of problems: psychological and career-related; and as you can imagine, the approach taken during the therapy/coaching will depend on which one it is. The sessions can either be a one time only or a continuous practice and, like CBT, they can be done in person or online and individually or in a group. There will not be a need of a lot of input from the client's end since in NLP it is often said that the coach gets all the information that they need from very few sentences.

When we talk about coaching, the ultimate goal is for people to become the masters of their own mind and, when you decide you are going to do an NLP training, you can choose which level you want to reach, from the most basic one to the one that allows you to officially start teaching others about the practice. When the sessions have a therapeutic goal, they tackle the problem and help fix it by reframing the person's map of reality.

Nowadays, if you do an online research for "NLP Coach" you will get numerous results. Amidst all of those, it is important that you know what to look for in an NLP professional, to ensure that you do not end up being scammed. This is something that inevitably happens when a certain practice become popular, but you should not let it push you away from trying NLP if it seems like it could help you reach your objectives.

What To Look For In an NLP Coach

An NLP coach is a type of life coach. When choosing yours, it is crucial that you do the proper research (keep in mind, though, that if you try coach A and do not like them, you can always try coach B or C. Yes, I am going to repeat it - there is no such thing as failure, only feedback). So, this is what you should think of in your mission to find the perfect NLP coach for yourself:

- Ask them to tell you their certification. You will want someone who is legit and is there anything more legit than an official certification? A certified coach might be more expensive, but if you are truly set on giving NLP a try, in the long run and considering what you will learn, it will be worth the investment.

- Check if their area of expertise and your area of need are a match.

- Make sure there is a good connection. A good NLP coach will put an effort into building a rapport with you before you start the work itself. If the person and their method don't make you feel comfortable enough to be honest and open up, there is no point in moving forward with them.

The First Session

The main goal of the first NLP session will be to build rapport with the client. The coach will go over your basic information (name, age, address, and so on), although they might know that data prior to the appointment, in case you two had a call before, which is a regular practice; as well as some details that are relevant to have a generic idea of what is your desired outcome of the coaching and how they can plan out the sessions to assist you into achieving that. So, expect questions like:

- What brought you here? What are you struggling with?

- What is your final goal for this coaching? What do you want to change?

- Have you tried other kinds of therapy or coaching for this goal?

- How long have you been struggling with this?

- What consequences does this have in your life?

- Do you believe there is a deeper reason for you to feel this way?

Don't worry if your answers are vague or if you simply don't have them: your continuous work will help you find (and define) them. Besides this questionnaire, the coach will explain what NLP is in greater detail than the research you did online and, in a general manner, how it can help you with your issue. From the information you give them, the coach might have an idea of what kind of NLP exercises he or she will suggest for you in subsequent sessions, although the final treatment plan will probably not be disclosed to you until a few sessions from this one. Another topic that will probably be mentioned in this first session is the confidentiality: the NLP will do his or her best to make you feel safe, and knowing that what you share will not leave those four walls is always comforting.

The Following Sessions

Soon you will start your exercises, but first, it is essential that your coach understands what happens during your Communication Model, how you get to your Internal Representations and how all of that is preventing you from exploring your full potential. With that information, the coach will be able to develop an exercise plan for you and your needs that will ultimately lead you to re-construct that model.

Don't expect to have to talk too much during these sessions, especially about things you are not at peace with and don't feel comfortable sharing. Rather, be prepared for plenty of visualization and imagination exercises that you might find to be fun. If you have been doing some research on NLP, you may have even heard or read people comparing this practice to hypnosis. It does make sense: NLP believes that success is all about your mind and how you control it and that having a positive or negative mindset greatly influences if you will get a positive or a negative outcome. Therefore, there is no better way of empowering a person than by getting to their unconscious and doing mind exercises that might even make them drift away. However, the tools and methods used in NLP and in hypnosis are different, and during an NLP session both the conscious and the unconscious are involved, while during a session of hypnosis only the unconscious mind is involved, so you get into a complete trance. As I mentioned earlier, when you finish your NLP sessions, you should be the master of your mind and have a manual of instructions figured out for your brain, so the exercises will revolve a lot around that.

Practicing NLP By Yourself

You can opt for learning NLP by yourself, as

there is a big amount of digital and physical resources that can guide you through the process and just like with CBT, not everyone has the financial means to have a coach and good coaches are not everywhere. Now, first off, you should know that if you do choose to practice NLP by yourself, you might face one big challenge, which is the fact that you will have to play two very different roles during the process. You will have to be the client, whose unconscious, thoughts and behaviors are being analyzed, as well as the coach, who is the guide of the sessions. It will be like you have to get out of yourself, which is something that not everyone can do, especially if the problem they are trying to solve is complex, like a depression or a panic disorder, for example.

Now, with all that in mind and accepting that possible challenge, if you still want to go ahead with this option, the logic will be the same as if you had a therapist. Whichever book or online platform you decide to have as the guide to your

DIY Neuro-Linguistic Programming adventure will explain what steps you should take and which exercises you can try. If it doesn't, it might not be the best choice of a book or platform. Like I have said before, research is essential, so look for reviews and information before you spend your money!

In case you are choosing to do NLP by yourself because you can't afford to have continuous therapy with a coach, it might be useful to know that a lot of NLP professionals do a free "trial", which might be a call or even an on-site session. So a good option would be to find a coach that seems like the best one for your case and go to their trial consultation. It will not be the same as actually doing an ongoing coaching program, but it will probably give you some lights on what you should focus on and what kind of approach you should go for. If the coach shares with you what kind of plan they would define for your case had you chosen to have more sessions, you can combine that information with the book or website you are using as your guide and it will be very beneficial. As great as those resources are, they are always somewhat generic, so having some information from a professional that was specifically tailored for you will be a plus. Next, I will talk about five NLP techniques that you can do at home, so keep on reading.

Chapter 3: Examples of Techniques

6 CBT Techniques

There are countless CBT techniques and exercises that therapists swear by. Each of them is more efficient for different types of mental health conditions but they all have the same foundation: that behaviors originate from thoughts, so if you can manage negative thoughts, you can change negative behaviors. Next, I will explain in detail six commonly used CBT practices, that your therapist might suggest for your situation or that you can try to do at home.

Calm Breathing

Calm Breathing, also known as Diaphragmatic Breathing, is a common technique in Cognitive Behavioral Therapy and it is very helpful for anxiety and panic attacks. As the name suggests, it is a series of breathing exercises where the goal is to put the individual in a calmer state. Often when someone feels anxious, their body fills itself with adrenaline and oxygen to prepare them to run away from whatever is threatening them (which can be something like picking up a phone or meeting someone new - it does not have to be a shark or a bear ready to attack you). Since the person is not actually going to run away, they will not be using all the oxygen being produced, and that is what causes their breathing to speed up, sometimes to the point of hyperventilation. It can be extremely difficult to go back to a normal breathing speed, which is why knowing a breathing exercise is really useful for people who suffer from certain mental health issues.

The Calm Breathing technique consists of only 3 steps that you should do in a comfortable seated position, with a hand on your stomach to feel it going in and out during the course of action:

1. Breathe slowly through your nose into your lower belly.

2. Hold the breath for 2 to 4 seconds.

3. Exhale for 4 seconds through your mouth.

You should repeat this process 6 to 8 times and wait for a couple of seconds in between each breathing cycle. Try to do this once or twice a day - you don't need to be feeling nervous, remember that at this point you are just practicing for moments of actual anxiety. If you want to take that extra step, you can even choose a couple of positive, relaxing quotes to tell yourself while you're doing the breathing exercises.

Realistic Thinking

I don't think there is one human being on Earth who has never had negative, unrealistic thoughts cross their mind. "Everybody hates me", "I am not good enough", "I am going to fail": we have all had moments of insecurity and disquiet before, but eventually, with time, encouragement of others and/or the power of our minds, we snap out of it, and that is perfectly normal. However for some people, these pessimistic thinking patterns are so regular and intense, that they turn into their reality - and that is when the situation becomes worrisome. When you find yourself in this gloomy thinking cycle, you start feeling anxious and sad for reasons that don't exist and that can lead to more serious psychological problems and risky behaviors.

With Realistic Thinking, the individual becomes aware of the harmful thoughts, confronts them and shifts them into positive ones. This exercise has 4 steps, it can be done anywhere, as long as you can concentrate and really commit to it and you can either do it all in your head, by talking to yourself or by writing down what you believe to be relevant, and that way keep up with the progress in your journal.

1. Answer the questions, "What are the negative thoughts I'm having?", "What is triggering these thoughts?" and "What do I believe is going to happen?"

2. From those answers, pinpoint which ones

are plausible (like being sad over a breakup, for example) and which ones you need to challenge. These will be the thoughts that, if you try to be rational and realistic, are so negative that they don't really make sense - the so-called thinking traps (that I will go more into ahead, in the chapter about Cognitive Distortions).

3. Focus on those thinking traps and figure out how you can look at them from the other perspective - the positive one. There are two sides to every coin and being able to see the positive side is a matter of practice. The key here is to internalize that just because you think it, it doesn't mean it is true.

4. Come up with a more balanced version of those thoughts and with mantras that will help you cope when the anxiety and negative feelings come up again.

So a practical example of this technique would

be:

Awareness of negative thought: I was invited to a birthday dinner tomorrow, but I feel really anxious because I only know the person who invited me and I know the other people will not like me and I will feel excluded.

Is it a realistic or unrealistic thought? It is normal to feel nervous about meeting new people, but, if I stop and really think about it, believing that no one at a dinner party will like me is an exaggeration. I feel this way because I have always been shy, but it should not stop me from celebrating an important date with a friend. So this is an unrealistic thought that I should confront.

How can I challenge this thought? Even if my brain tells me so, it is impossible for me to know for sure that nobody will like me. This is not a fact, it is just my brain playing tricks on me. Even if the small chances of nobody liking me did happen, my friend invited me to the party because our relationship is important to them and I should honor that instead of focusing on other people.

What can I do to cope with the nerves?
Every time the anxiety starts, I will take a deep breath and repeat to myself "My friend will be happy that I am by their side on their birthday. I will just be myself and I will most likely meet nice, like-minded people. I will have a great night!"

Pleasant Activity Scheduling
Doing things you like is a great way of feeling more relaxed, even if it is only while you are doing it, and that is the simple reason why Pleasant Activity Scheduling is an effective way of feeling better and, therefore, behaving better.

If you can afford it and if there is any activity going on where you live that seems interesting, enroll in it. If you like exercising, go to the gym; if you like to sing, join a choir; if you enjoy helping other people, start volunteering! This way you will already have a schedule set up and the fact that you are spending your money on it is an extra incentive to actually do it.

Another option is to buy a calendar or download a calendar app on your phone and make your own schedule of an activity. 30 minutes of gardening, 1 hour of painting, 2 hours of yoga, whatever makes you feel good!

This might seem like a very basic technique, but studies have proved that it can be very successful. One example of this is a study where there were created 17 activity categories (including "physical activity (32%), medication management (22%), active-non-physical (19%) and passive (14%) activities"[6]) that 597 individuals with depression were involved in for a year. After the 12 months, they concluded that social activities and instrumental activities, in particular, can be

---

[6] Riebe G., Fan, M., Unützer J. & Vannoy S. (2012). Activity scheduling as a core component of effective care management for late-life depression. - PubMed - NCBI. [online] Available at: https://www.ncbi.nlm.nih.gov/pubmed/22367982 [Accessed 18 Mar. 2019].

beneficial to those suffering from depression.

Progressive Muscle Relaxation (PMR)

When someone is constantly anxious, some symptoms are so frequent that, after a while, they become normal and the individual stops noticing them. This is quite common with muscle tension that, just like the shortness of breath I have talked about before, happens as a reaction of the body to something that is considered a threat. The exercise of Progressive Muscle Relaxation allows the person to train the body and make it remember what it feels like to have the muscles relaxed. It is an exercise of contrast, where you purposely go from tense to relaxed to tense, and so on. Take 10 to 20 minutes once or twice a week and follow these steps, from muscle group to muscle group (you can do it from the bottom to the top: feet, lower legs, thighs, stomach, back, hands, arms, shoulders, neck, jaw, and forehead. When there is a pair, work on one side at a time, i.e. first left hand and then right hand):

1. Put on comfortable clothes, take off your

shoes, go to a quiet room and find a comfortable position to be in during the exercise: you can lie down or sit in a comfortable armchair, preferably one you can recline. During the exercise, beware of any injuries you might have: you will want to be careful not to worsen them and in case of severe injuries, you might even want to contact your doctor to make sure you don't do anything harmful. As you can see, comfort is the keyword for this technique.

2. Do some minutes of the Calm Breathing exercise I mentioned above, just to put you in a more relaxed state.

3. Now, let's say you start with your feet. Take a deep breath in and tighten your feet muscles for 5 to 10 seconds (be careful not to make them too tense, or you can hurt yourself. There is no need to push yourself too hard).

4. Then relax your feet muscles suddenly, so that you really feel the difference, and exhale at the same time.

5. After 10 to 15 seconds, move on to the next muscle group.

At first, step number 3 might feel a little bit uncomfortable but with time, it will get easier and when you feel like you've got it, you can start to gather muscle groups (i.e., instead of doing forehead, then jaw, you can do your entire face at the same time). This exercise is great for people of all ages - even for children - and for both psychological and physical issues, and it can even be beneficial for healthy individuals: a lot of people work in a seated position in front of a computer 8 hours a day, 5 days a week (if not more!), and that causes a lot of tension to accumulate without them even realizing. If you choose to do this by yourself and feel like you need some guidance to start, there are a lot of great videos online and mobile apps you can download and, in case you are not sure how to tighten each muscle group, here is a generic guide:

- Feet: curl your toes.

- Lower legs: pull your toes up, towards yourself.

- Thighs: squeeze the muscles.

- Arms: make the movement as if you were showing your arm muscle to someone.

- Hands: make a fist and squeeze.

- Stomach: take a deep breath in and only exhale after those 5 to 10 seconds.

- Back: push your shoulder blades back, towards each other.

- Shoulders: push your shoulders up, as if they were trying to touch your ears.

- Neck: put your face forward and slowly start looking up, moving your neck.

- Jaw: open your mouth as much as you can.

- Forehead: raise your eyebrows as high as you can.

Exposure

When you fear something, you naturally avoid it. An important part of CBT is for the individual to face their fears and by doing so, become desensitized to them and learn how to manage the feelings that occur from those fears, which is, in a simplified manner, what the method of Exposure consists of. Everybody is scared of something but some people feel such intense fears that they become paralyzing and controlling of their lives - such as phobias, obsessive-compulsive disorders, and PTSD - and that is when it is important to intervene, which you can do by following these steps:

1. Get your journal and write down your fears in an order, so that you can figure out which ones are more intense - the so-

called fear or exposure hierarchy.

2. Figure out ways of exposing yourself to them. You can start with the least intense fear (Graded or Gradual Exposure) or with the most intense one (Flooding), and you can combine the Exposure with relaxation techniques (Systematic Desensitization). The degree of exposure can increase throughout time, as you start feeling more and more comfortable with it. If you were scared of bees, for example, you could start by simply looking at a photo or video of some bees, and gradually work on it until you felt capable of going on an apiary visit.

3. Do it regularly, at your own pace, until you don't feel the anxiety from that fear anymore.

There are three big types of Exposure therapy:

- **In Vivo Exposure**, where the person is facing their fears in real life. Using the bee example again: if you went on a visit to an apiary, you would be doing In Vivo Exposure.

- **Imaginal Exposure**, where the person faces their fears in their head, by comprehensively imagining the situation. So here you would not actually go to an apiary, but you would picture the visit in your head.

- **VR Exposure**, a more recent technique where the therapist (or you) uses technology to make you feel like you are in a real-life situation. You would not go on a beekeeping visit, but you would use a VR headset to simulate one.

Two aspects that you should never ignore if you opt for the Exposure method are:

- **Your limit.** I have mentioned before that a CBT therapist will never put someone in a situation where they don't feel comfortable, so if you go to a professional, all you have to do is be open and honest about how you feel. If you choose to try Exposure by yourself, you are your own therapist and you should still follow that "rule".

- **Danger**, particularly if you do it by yourself. If you are scared of heights, don't try to dangle from the balcony of the 50th floor of a building. Don't ever put yourself in risky situations and keep in mind that it is normal to have fears, so as long as they don't have a major impact in your quality of life, there is no need to purposely expose yourself to them.

Mindfulness

This one you have probably heard about before, even if you did not see it being related to CBT. Mindfulness is a very popular practice nowadays and, when it is used as a part of CBT, it is commonly referred to as MiCBT (Mindfulness-integrated Cognitive Behavior Therapy).

Mindfulness is a Buddhist technique, that originated in India a long, long time ago in a meditation type called Vipassana, which means "insight into the true nature of reality". It consists of living in the present and being mindful of what is happening right now. It might sound simple, but most of us do not live in the now. We constantly daydream, worry about the future and relive the past in our minds (particularly our negative past experiences), which has a harmful impact in our present state. In mindfulness, we are aware of our feelings and emotions and we let them naturally come and go, accepting the fact that impermanence - the fact that everything, including our emotions, is in constant change - is a natural thing and becoming less strict with our own selves. We focus on the present moment and we do not judge.

There is one exercise that sums up pretty well what mindfulness is about and it is called "The Raisin Exercise" (although it could be called "The [insert any food that has a unique feel to it, a unique taste or a unique smell] Exercise"). It can be suggested to you during your sessions with the therapist, but it is also very easy to do at home, so you can even do it right after you read the instructions and get a better understanding of how mindfulness can help you. There are 3 steps to this exercise:

1. Grab a raisin (or whatever food you decided to go for).

2. Pay attention to it. Bring your focus to how the raisin feels on your hand, if it has any particular smell when you bring it to your nose and breathe in slowly, how it feels and tastes in your mouth, from the moment you put on your tongue, to the moment you start chewing to the moment you swallow it.

3. Take a deep and slow breath.

Do you see what happened? You just ate a raisin and were fully in the moment throughout the entire process. Now, I know eating a raisin could not be a simpler thing to do. But imagine applying these three steps to other moments in your daily life, bigger, more complex moments. When you do something and you are fully involved in it, your brain does not even remember that it could be using that time to stress out about something (that a lot of times is not even worth stressing out about) instead.

Now that you are more familiar with the concept of mindfulness applied to a simple event, you can proceed to explore the technique of MiCBT. It has 4 stages and it teaches you how to be aware of your personal, internal experiences, as well as the ones happening around you.

Personal Stage

The first stage typically lasts one month. During this month, you pay attention to your own body and mind. You focus on your posture, your gestures, your muscles; you learn how to prevent dysfunctional thoughts; how to regulate your emotions; how your body and your mind relate and influence each other; how to detach yourself from thinking patterns that are preventing you from moving on and growing. During this stage, you become mindful of your own self.

Exposure Stage

On the second stage, you overcome your fears. I have talked about the method of Exposure before, so you can imagine how this step goes. The goal here is to apply what you learn in stage 1 to real life experiences you were purposely avoiding up until that point. You apply mindfulness to personal situations of distress.

Interpersonal Stage

Stage 3 is about communication. You learn how to keep calm in tense situations with others and how to properly make your point come across without letting your emotions get the best of you and make you act irrationally; you become more patient and understanding of how the other person might be feeling, as well as what they might be thinking, making stressful situations less stressful. You apply mindfulness to situations of distress with others.

Empathic Stage

On the final stage, you become compassionate and empathetic towards others. You see the bigger picture and start looking at problems as something relative. You have learned how to be kind and how to naturally control yourself in situations where you would normally act out of impulse. You are at peace, you feel a stronger, deeper connection with yourself and others and your whole life is now a mindful experience.

Practicing mindfulness can be beneficial for everybody, even for people who are not looking for therapy to treat their mental illness, because chances are they do not live in the present. And isn't the present and what we do in the now the most important thing? And for those who struggle with their mental health, mindfulness can be of great use, since it teaches us how to stop and enjoy the now. It gives people more joy of living and makes them put things into perspective. What is this thing that usually makes me anxious in the big scheme of life and when there are so many smalls things in my life that I can enjoy and put my body and soul into every single day?

6 NLP Techniques

As you know by now, a lot of the techniques used in NLP will make you visualize situations. They are like imagination games, that all have the same final goal: for the person to discover a structure that they have used in situations of success and that they can reproduce in other areas that they do not excel at (yet), giving them the power of being in control of their life. The techniques that will work for your situation depend on your desired outcome, which can be of a professional nature or of a therapeutic one (I will get into that in the next chapter, when I talk about the benefits of NLP). So you can imagine the variety of exercises there are!

Meta Model

We start with a complex one, in the sense that there are quite a few subconcepts to the concept of the Meta Model. Remember the Distortion, Deletion and Generalization that I talked about in the chapter about the NLP Communication Model? I mentioned that these processes could be useful, but they can also be limiting. The Meta Model is composed by 13 verbal patterns, also known as violations of the Meta Model, and that consist of ways in which the person might be distorting, deleting or generalizing information in a restraining manner. They are all different but they can all be solved by doing the same thing: questioning the veracity of the statement. The 13 verbal patterns of the Meta Model are:

Deletions

Simple Deletions

Simple Deletions happen when an important part of a statement is not specified, jeopardizing its meaning. A lot of times, this violation happens because we assume the other person is aware of what we are talking about and so, there is no need to be specific, and it happens so often that a lot of the times we don't even notice it. Every time you use the words "it" and "that", there is a Simple Deletion. Now of course it does not cause confusion every single time, for example, if your friend has a dress on her hands and asks "Is it pretty?" you know by context that she is talking about the dress; and sometimes it just sparks a question and is it solved, "Can you pass me that juice?" "The orange one?" "Yes". But it can sure be the root of a lot of misunderstandings.

The way of solving this with the Meta Model is by asking questions, in order to get those missing details. The Simple Deletions can be of four types:

Unspecified Nouns

In a statement with an unspecified noun, what is missing is the subject, so the person does not understand what the sentence is talking about.

"That is a tricky situation." What is a tricky situation?

Unspecified Adjectives

"Katy only goes for guys who are jerks". So we know that Katy does not have the best of luck in her love life, but in what way are these guys jerks? What do they do that qualifies them as such? The adjective here is not specific enough and we do not get the full story.

Unspecified Referential Index

When the listener does not get information as to who the "Who" of the sentence is. "They are going to take us on a tour this evening". Who are they and who are us? "The guides of the hotel are going to take our trip group on a tour this evening" would be a more complete sentence.

Unspecified Verbs

And finally, a case of Unspecified Verb happens when there is not enough information about the "What" of the sentence. You use a verb but the sentence as a whole is not specific enough for the listener to get what actually happened. "She aced it!". Well... we know she did excellent, but at what and how? The sentence is too generic and the person on the other side will not get the full meaning. "She aced her English test, she got an A!". Now, that is more like it!

Nominalizations

Nominalization qualifies as a Deletion violation in the sense that a verb is turned into a noun and it causes the statement to partially lose its meaning. This might be a little bit confusing, but I will clarify it with a commonly used example: the word "relationship". A relationship is a process of relating to someone, and the keyword there is process. What relating to someone means to person A can be completely different than what it means to person B. That causes different expectations, different behaviors and a lot of misunderstandings. That is why the key to a healthy relationship is communication, although... communication is another case of a nominalization. You can get around nominalizations by asking for details about the processes that have been turned into nouns. Talk about what it means for you to relate to someone, and what it means for your partner, and that will avoid future confusions.

Comparisons

Comparisons, or Null Comparatives, are an extra type of Simple Deletions and they happen when you phrase a statement as if it was going to be a comparison (oftentimes with the use of comparatives, like "better", "taller, "colder", and so on), but don't follow through with the comparison, which does not leave the other person anything to measure up with and get a better idea of what you are really trying to express. If you tell me "I am more confident now", you have gotten more confident but I do not fully get the idea you mean to convey. So the key here would be to ask you "than when?": you are more confident than when?

Distortions

Lost Performative

Lost Performative consists of rules or value judgements about the self or others that do not have a real author (which is why they are sometimes considered another type of Simple Deletions - there is a part of the meaning that is not properly conveyed). It is when either a positive or a negative remark is made about something - often in the form of a suggestion - but it is not explicit regarding who did it or if there is proof of its legitimacy. So, an example of this could be "That haircut does not give you a professional look and you will not be able to get a job". The Meta Model challenges this verbal pattern by asking who says that. Who says that a certain hairdo is not professional and what makes that the actual reality?

Complex Equivalence

A Complex Equivalence states the relationship between two things, situations or thoughts, that

A=B, even though there is no proof of this connection. "My friend has not called me since he moved back to the city, that means he doesn't like me anymore". How many times have you assumed someone is not interested in keeping in touch with you because they have not tried to reach you? And how many times have you found out that they were actually really busy with a project or that they were helping a loved one in times of need or... any other reason than the one you assumed?

You made a Complex Equivalence that could have cost you your friendship and the way that the Meta Model would have prevented that would be by asking if A always means B, or if it is possible that it could mean C. In that case, the Model would have made you think of other options why your friend has not called you, and maybe even make you be the one reaching out to them first.

Presuppositions

A Presupposition happens when one part of a statement is omitted and so it must be pre-assumed for the statement to make sense. They are considered to be the Meta Model violation that is harder to recognize and one of the most common ones in human communication, which is why it is important for the NLP student to practice how to be aware of them and how to solve them, no matter how difficult it might be at first. There are two elements that NLP considers in Presuppositions: the surface structure, which is the information we specifically give when we make a statement and refers to the conscious brain; and the deep structure, which is the meaning of the statement that is not said but is supposed to be read somewhere between the lines and refers to the unconscious brain. Consider the sentence, "Joshua lived in the city for a long time". What you just read is the surface structure and the deep structure would consist of details like which city and for how long, that you cannot find out through that statement.

Presuppositions can be simple or complex and I will give you examples of both:

- A Simple Presupposition is when the existence of something or someone is presupposed. For example when I say "My sister is going to Spain", you presuppose the existence of my sister.

- A Complex Presupposition is when you have to presuppose more than a simple existence. When I say "I have a better computer now", you presuppose I used to have another computer that was not as good. Or if I say "Who cares if the food is expensive", you presuppose no one cares that the food is expensive.

As is the case with a lot of the other verbal patterns I am listing, not every Presupposition is harmful. The example I gave for the Simple Presupposition, for instance, would probably not cause any problems. I talk about my sister and you believe I have a sister. But it is not always that simple.

Let's take the statement "What Margaret said was offensive" as an example. In it, you can find Simple Presuppositions, like the fact that there is a person called Margaret, as well as Complex ones, like the fact that what she said offended someone. The Meta Model challenges you to assess how much truth there is to the Presuppositions. So in this case, the Simple Presuppositions would be fine, but regarding the second one you could ask "Who was it offensive for and why?". Doing this exercise of questioning Presuppositions - particularly the Complex ones - can be very beneficial for the improvement of your communication skills, as you become more aware of others' reality maps and thinking patterns, consequently getting a better understanding of their behaviors.

Mind Reading

Quite self-explanatory, a mind reading happens when you believe you know what's going through someone's mind, even though they did not say or do anything to prove it. Mind reading can happen in 3 ways:

- When you believe you know yours or someone else's future. An example would be "I know I will not get the job".

- When you assume you know what the other person is thinking or feeling. An example would be "I am sorry to annoy you with my problems", when you are venting to someone.

- When you assume the other person knows how you are feeling or what you are thinking. A common example is when you are in love with a friend who doesn't reciprocate the feeling, "You know how I feel about you!"

The Meta Model solves this violation by asking " Is there actual evidence of what you are assuming?"

Cause and Effect

This verbal pattern happens when you justify an internal process, i.e. the way you are feeling or thinking (the Effect) with an external event (the Cause) that actually did not result in the Effect. How many times, for example, have you heard or said the sentence, "The Winter weather makes me feel depressed". It is not literally the weather that makes you feel this way, but something deeper, and NLP defends that because according to the practice, you are in charge of the way you feel and think because you are the one who gives positive or negative meanings to all external stimuli, so external events can't have that kind of impact on your state. The way that the Meta Model solves this violation is by asking for more details about this Cause and Effect. How exactly does the Winter weather make you feel that way? Why? What could you do to feel better about the cold and rain?

Generalizations

Modal Operators

You probably learned in English classes what modal verbs are. They are verbs that express obligation, ability, permission or possibility (must and must not, can and cannot, should and should not, may or may not are some of them) and they are the cause to this violation. Modal Operators can be of two main kinds: of Necessity and of Possibility.

A Modal Operator of Necessity is a sentence that implies obligation, almost like a rule, when there is no choice. Whatever is said has to happen. Some commonly used verbs are "must" and "have to", so an example would be "I must lose weight". When this is said, we all understand that the person has no option but to lose weight. The Meta Model challenges this violation by asking what would be the consequences if whatever has to happen did not happen and from there, figure out if what they are saying is true or not. Someone who is curvy and is putting too much pressure on themselves to lose weight might realize that if they do not lose weight, no real damaging consequences will happen; while someone who is obese and whose weight is threatening their life might realize that they must actually lose weight if they want to improve their wellbeing.

A Modal Operator of Possibility is when the statement mentions something that may or may not happen so, contrary to the Modal Operators of Necessity, these ones offer choices. But they can also be used in a way that implies that the person has several choices, but does not have what it takes to choose the one that would be considered the best. Some commonly used verbs are "could" and "can" and an example would be, "I can't go on a 3 hour hike". In this case, the Meta Model would lead you to ask why - Why can't you do the hike? What stops you from being able to do it? - and, again, assess the truthfulness in your statement, as well if there is something you can change to turn the "can't" into a "can". If you did this exercise and came to the conclusion that you can't do the hike because you do not have appropriate shoes, you could solve it by buying a pair or borrowing from a friend.

Universal Quantifiers

It is a generalization about people and events, often done by using the words "Everybody", "Nobody", "Every time" and "Never", with no referential index. "Everybody thinks I am pathetic", for instance, does not specify who is everybody but we know that is not literally every single person in the world. So, who is the person who said that is referring to? This kind of verbal pattern is an exaggeration of reality and can be challenged simply by assessing if when someone says "always", they actually mean every single time, when they say "nobody" they actually mean zero people, an so on.

Anchoring

If you consult the Merriam-Webster dictionary, you find that an anchor is "a device usually of metal attached to a ship or boat by a cable and cast overboard to hold it in a particular place by means of a fluke that digs into the bottom"[7]. When you use Anchoring methods in NLP, you find responses (which can be positive or negative) that you can use every time you find yourself in similar situations (which can be internal, such as a thought, or external, such as someone's touch on your skin) and that can help you stabilize the way you feel and behave, much like a physical anchor stabilizes a boat on the sea. So, when the stimulus X happens, you have the response Y - with the anchoring process, Y can purposefully or naturally become an easy and quick response for every time the trigger X (the anchor) happens. This may remind you of the Pavlov experiment with the dogs and it is, indeed, commonly compared to it.

When an NLP Coach uses Anchoring techniques, their goal is to practice the connection between anchor A and response B (that is a positive

---

[7] (n.d.). Anchor | Definition of Anchor by Merriam-Webster. [online] Available at: https://www.merriam-webster.com/dictionary/anchor [Accessed 18 Mar. 2019].

response), so that ultimately it becomes automatic for the person. These anchors must be specific, periodic, intense and related to one single unique response in order for the exercise to work.

In NLP, there are three types of Anchors connected to three of our five senses, that can be used individually or combined:

- Visual Anchors, for example if you had a small token with you at all times, that you could look at to trigger a positive feeling (external visual anchor); or a friend you can think of for the same purpose (internal visual anchor).

- Auditory Anchors, like a snap sound you can make with your fingers (external auditory anchor) or the voice of someone you can imagine (internal auditory anchor).

- Kinesthetic Anchors, like a gesture you can

make (external kinesthetic anchor) or imagining someone giving you a hug (internal kinesthetic anchor).

So, the basic Anchoring process is done in 4 steps and it takes practice and repetition for you to lay the anchor. Let's say you want an anchor for the feeling of relaxation:

1. First, you need to think of a moment in your life where you felt truly relaxed. If you are with a Coach, you will be asked to tell the story of that moment; if you are doing the exercise by yourself, you can either say it out loud or simply replay it in your head with as much detail as you can. As long as you can recall the way you felt in that situation, that is the most important part.

2. Then, you establish the anchor. For example, you can choose an auditory/kinesthetic anchor: snapping your fingers. What you need to do is snap

your fingers and think of the moment again and, when you feel at the peak of your relaxation, let go, release the trigger.

3. After a bit, you should repeat that process with another event where you felt truly relaxed.

4. Then, it is time to test the anchor. Think of a third time when you felt relaxed and check the clock to see how long it takes for it to fire the anchor. In this step, figure out how strong the anchor-feeling connection is and if there is a need for more repetition of steps 1 and 2.

From the moment the anchor is properly laid and internalized, in future situations, you can snap your fingers when you start feeling anxious, triggering your brain into turning the anxiety into relaxation. You can start feeling good on demand whenever you want to!

Another Anchoring process is the one where a person turns a negative anchor into a positive one, practicing to the point where they can go from one to the other in a matter of minutes. This process is called Chaining Anchoring and it can be done by thinking of the event that triggers the negative response, choose a positive feeling to substitute the negative one, define the steps you will take to gradually go from negative to positive, repeating as many times as possible until you do not feel bad about the event anymore. Here is an example: I compare myself negatively to others > I get angry at myself for wasting time doing it, instead of putting effort into improving myself > I get excited thinking about all the things I can do > I stop comparing and start doing.

Representational System Discovery

The Representational System Discovery is a test to find out which of the five senses a person uses the most to understand and process what is going on around them. We use all or most of our senses but all of us also have an inclination to interpret the world and decode information with a specific one: some of us are more visual, others respond better to auditory stimuli, others need the touch component to get a better understanding of something, and so on. Whichever sense we get as a result on the test is our Preferred Representational System.

There are several resources online where you can easily take this test, but with NLP, you can learn how to find your own Preferred Representational System, otherwise known as Preferred Sensory Channel, without having to take the test, as well as other people's. The way one reacts, moves and talks say a lot about which sense they use the most (which is more often than not the visual, the auditory or the kinesthetic. The olfactory and gustatory are not as relevant for this technique) and this can be useful in several ways. When you know your own preferred system, you get a better idea of how you can go about improving skills and learning new ones. When you know another person's preferred system, you can more effectively communicate with them.

You can discover someone's Preferred Representational System by observing and listening. For example, let's say you put a dog in front of two people. One immediately pets it and the other one simply observes and takes a photo of the animal. This situation gives us a clue into which of the five senses the two people prefer: kinesthetic for the first one and visual for the second one. Another example would be two people talking about an idea they had that they believe to be great. One says "Can you see how well it would work?", while the other one says "Doesn't my idea sound great?" In this case, you would relate the visual sense to the first person and the auditory sense to the second one.

Perceptual Positions

Sometimes, when something bad happens, we continue to feel negative emotions even after the situation happened. Like when we hold a grudge towards someone or when we feel embarrassed recalling a previous awkward moment. We have all been there. The exercise of Perceptual

Positions teaches us the skill of being aware of more than our own point of view on a situation. By doing this, the person becomes less inclined to be harsh on themselves and on other people, which can be a really useful tool to increase one's self-confidence, self-love and self-awareness and to improve existing relationships, as well as building new ones in a healthy manner. So, how can you do this?

In Perceptual Positions, there are four positions that you will try to imagine yourself in (the first three are the original ones, and the Fourth one was added to the list afterwards):

First Position

The First Position, also mentioned in NLP as a fully associated position, refers to your own perspective and your own filter systems. It happens when you remember something that happened in your life in the past or imagine yourself in a certain situation in the future; when you exclusively consider what you think, how you feel and what you want. When you do this imagination exercise, you don't see yourself. Instead, you see the way things happening around you would look like in your own eyes. Some people find it difficult to truly connect to their first - for example, people who constantly put other people's needs ahead of their own - while others have a hard time dissociating from it - for example, someone who suffers from an addiction.

Some questions you can make while you are in the First Position are:

- How did/do I feel?
- How did/do I react?
- What did/do I see/hear/smell?
- What was/is my take on what happened?

Second Position

The Second Position is when you put yourself in the shoes of another person, and look at the situation through their eyes. You consider how the situation would feel for them. So if the event was an interaction between a friend and yourself, imagining it from the Second Position means you would be looking to and hearing your First, and addressing it as "you".

It is important to mention that putting yourself in Second Position too often can be very harmful, because you end up putting yourself in a situation of dependency of the other person to make decisions, and that can even become dangerous. A very clear and very intense example of this is that of a person in an abusive relationship. Often, people in this situation are unable to escape because they have been brainwashed into always putting themselves in second and putting their partner's needs and wants before their own. On the other hand, not being able to do it at all is also not good, as others will start seeing you as a selfish person.

Some questions you can make while you are in the Second Position are:

- What do I feel when I put myself in the other person's shoes?

- How did they react and what are the possible reasons as to why?

- What were other ways they could have behaved and why do I think they didn't?

Third Position

The Third Position is when you imagine the situation as a third person who is not directly involved and who does not know anything about it - the neutral observer. So, in this imagination exercise, and considering the same example of the interaction between yourself and a friend, that is exactly who you would see: yourself and your friend and the whole situation taking place "in real time". It puts you in a position where you consider how you would look at it from the outside, almost as if you were watching a TV show. It offers a more objective perspective, which is a great source of feedback and insights you would not get while personally involved in the event.

Being able to assume the Third Position is a great tool if you choose to practice Neuro-Linguistic Programming by yourself (remember when we told you about the challenge of having to assume the role of your own coach/therapist? Here is the solution). However, there is a flip side to it and it can be a harmful position to stay in for a long period of time. A person who spends too much time in Third does not experience things in first hand, and ends up not really living their life, but merely observing it. This can deteriorate relationships with others, as the person will tend to drift away from them, and their own wellbeing and sense of self, since the person's motivation will decrease and that can have severe consequences on their mental health. People who spend too much time in Third Position tend to lose themselves.

The Third Position can be of three types: a Pure Third, who is a person not directly involved but who has been in your position and the other person's position before and, consequently, has some personal knowledge about both; the Meta, who is a person who is not involved but has been in your position before and has personal knowledge about it; and the Observer, who is not involved and does not have any personal knowledge about either of the positions.

Some questions you can make while you are in the Third Position are:

- What do you (the third person) see and hear?
- How does it make you feel?
- What advice would you give to both participants?

Fourth Position

When you assume the Fourth Position, you look at the situation as a whole, with the First, Second and Third positions in the picture at the same time. So here there would not be an "I", a "You" or a "She/He", but a "We". It refers to the collective and considers what is of best interest for it. Someone who decides to stop using single-use plastic because it is the right thing to do for humanity as a whole is putting themselves in the Fourth Position. They see the First - themselves -, the Second - Earth (it does not always have to be a person) - and the Third (everyone else on Earth), they find common ground between the three and make their own judgement on what is best for all parties. This is a position of great importance for people heavily involved with volunteering programs, for people who live to take care of their loved ones and for people committed to a religion. Per contra, someone who does not feel like they fit in in any group or community might have a hard time doing the same thing, as well as someone who is not yet able to put themselves in all of the previous mentioned positions.

Now that you are familiar with the four positions

and you have read some examples of all of them, it is probably clear for you to understand how being able to put yourself in all of them can be beneficial. It makes it easier for you to build rapport with others and to effectively communicate with them; it helps you get a sharper sense of self and understand when you were in the right and in the wrong; it is a great tool to use when you want to set goals for yourself, by imagining your First in the desired future situation; it can give you a more objective and less emotional take on an event you were involved in; and it can lead you to make a decision that is beneficial for not only yourself, but an entire group of people.

Rapport

Earlier in the ebook, I have talked about how important and valuable building a Rapport with someone can be. In case you forgot, the Rapport is a sense of harmony and acceptance between two people, when the differences between them are put to the side and the similarities are the focus, and that makes it easier for them to communicate and to relate to one another. As I have also said before, in some situations you build Rapport naturally, like when you develop an effortless friendship with someone, but in other situations you have to make it happen. In those cases, practicing NLP comes in handy. There are several techniques you can try, if you are looking to learn the skill of building Rapport even with people you disagree with. Here are two:

- **Mirroring**: to use this technique when you are talking to someone, imagine that there is a mirror between the two of you and that you are a reflection of them. Whatever they do, you repeat. You can make your breathing cycles match theirs, you can start talking in the same tone as them, you can adopt their posture and mimic gestures they make (keeping in mind that there is a mirror between you two, meaning that if the other person raises their left arm, you raise your right one), for instance. Doing this eases the process of meeting someone new but it should be natural and come from an honest desire to build a relationship with them. Otherwise, it will be nothing more than manipulation, which is not the goal.

- **Matching**: similar to Mirroring, it is also about mimicking, but doing it exactly as the other person does it. So if the person you are talking to raises their left arm, you also raise your left arm. This is something we do naturally, replicating other people's behavior, especially when we are with them often. One recurrent example of natural matching is when we spend so much time with someone, we start saying unusual expressions and words that they usually use. It happens in such a natural way that, when you become aware of it, it might even feel a little bit weird. Matching can also be done internally, when someone fully understands how you feel, has the same values as you and looks at the world through the same lenses.

When you do this type of exercises though, it is very important to know your limit, as building too much rapport might lead you to lose yourself and live to please others; and building rapport with too many people with negative views on life might ultimately lead you to have the same kind of perspective, which can have damaging consequences on your mental health.

Swish Pattern

To swish means to substitute a bad habit, such as smoking, nail biting and overeating, with a more useful one, creating a new and improved sense of self. If you ask someone who has got an addiction - let's use overeating as the example here - to think of themselves as doers of the harmful habit, as someone who cannot resist food and who lost total control over their diet - and to imagine themselves as non-doers - as someone with a balanced, healthy diet - more often than not you will find that if a person could choose in that exact moment which option they would want for their life, they would probably opt for the second one.

So, with the Swish Pattern technique, that is precisely what you do: you create, in your mind, an image of yourself that is not dependent on food and who feels so much better and is so much happier than you are right now. When you picture that better version of yourself, you feel motivated to fight your addiction and inspired to put in an effort to make that imagined self-image your actual reality. Beware though not to create an image of yourself that is unrealistic, as that will not work as motivation but as a reason for you to give up, because you will, sooner or later, realize that what you are trying to achieve is not attainable. When you create a better version of yourself in your mind, try to find a balance between inspiring and unrealistic.

The Swish Pattern has got 5 steps that you should repeat 5 to 10 times, each time you do it. Don't forget to break state - that is, to clear your mind - in between repetitions.

1. Identify the problem you are struggling with and create a big image in your mind of yourself doing the habit that you are trying to fight. Using the example above, you would create an image in your brain of yourself binge-eating unhealthy food and becoming out of shape.

2. Understand what triggers you to engage in the habit. Why am I eating so much? What is causing me to have no control over food? By knowing the trigger, you will know when to apply the swish technique "in real life". When you clearly know what the trigger is, clear your brain for a couple of seconds, before you move on to the third step.

3. Put that image to the side and create an even bigger one of yourself where you do not feel the need to do that habit. This is

the image that should be both motivational and realistic. So you could imagine yourself eating well portioned, well balanced meals, rich in colorful fruits and vegetables, just like those you see on YouTube and Instagram, that slowly bring you back to a healthy shape. Locate where and what that image makes you feel, give that feeling a color, and make it brighter and more intense.

4. Now, bring back the first image you created, so that you have both images present in your mind. Make the bad one big, full of color and closer to you; and the good one small, with dull colors and far away from you.

5. Finally, swap them around. Make the image of that you want to get rid of small and grey and throw it as far away from you as you can; and make the one of your final goal big and bright and make it come closer to you as fast as you can. You can

also imagine sounds to make this swap even more intense. Associate with the new image and allow yourself to take your time and to feel amazing as you see this improved version of yourself. You just swished!

Chapter 4: Benefits

What are CBT's Main Benefits?

As quoted before, Cognitive Behavioral Therapy can be helpful for various psychological issues, some already specified, such as PTSD, anxiety or depression. These issues arise when our brains start telling us lies and make us feel worried about things that are not really worrisome. In other words, when we start to have Cognitive Distortions.

Cognitive Distortions

It was the father of CBT, Aaron Beck, who first introduced the theory of the Cognitive Distortions in 1976, that was, later on in the 80s, picked up and studied by his student, Dr. David Burns, in his bestselling book "Feeling Good: The New Mood Therapy". In his book, Burns detailed 10 types of Cognitive Distortions, but throughout the years numerous more have been added to the list. Chances are you have felt at least one of these Cognitive Distortions before, but some people feel it in such a severe way that it becomes a big inhibitor to their happiness and good quality of life. In this ebook, I will talk about the 10 distortions that Burns first introduced, since they are still so relevant in today's reality.

Black and White thinking

When your brain can imagine the best case scenario and the worst case scenario, but nothing in between. The world is black and white and there is absolutely no grey. Now, we all have this thinking process from time to time, especially when we feel more down, angry or insecure. But when an individual's mind constantly works like this and sees everything in extremes, they more often than not ignore the most reasonable case scenarios, which happen to be the most likely ones to actually occur. This thought cycle can be extremely harmful to:

- One's view of themselves, either because they see themselves as the worst person on

Earth or the best one.

- One's relationships with others, because it becomes impossible to see them as regular human beings with both qualities and flaws and, for that reason, to keep healthy relationships with them.

- One's success in life: because they either believe everything will work just fine and put no effort into their tasks or that nothing will ever work, so there is no point in even trying. To be successful, you need to try.

An example of Black and White Thinking is "I will never be good enough to be chosen for a job, so I will not send any resumes."

Overgeneralization

When a person draws a generalized conclusion from one single occurrence. It happens when we can't deal with emotions that a certain situation causes in a healthy way, and so it ends up distorting the way we look at future similar situations. For someone with a tendency to overgeneralize, there is no need to try again: you try once and if you fail once, you will fail every time. It can prevent an individual from making new friends, from starting a fun hobby, from taking the next step in their career or from meeting the love of their life - simply because it did not work at the first attempt.

An example of an Overgeneralization is "I went to a yoga class and was not able to do the positions that the instructor was teaching, so I will never try yoga again."

Mental filters

When a person filters out information (that is usually negative). For people with this kind of cognitive distortion, the world would have to be perfect for them to be able to fully enjoy life. If everything is going well, except for one small detail - even if it is not a detail they can control - then, in this person's eyes, nothing is going well.

It is almost like an obsession to find and focus on the negative side of things. This is not realistic, merely because life is never perfect.

An example of a Mental filter would be if an artist posted one of their paintings online, got 20 comments - 19 positive ones and a negative one - and put all their focus on the single negative comment. This would lead to sadness and insecurity on their work, despite the fact that the majority of people were fans of the painting.

Discounting the positives

Similarly to the Mental Filters, when someone discounts the positives, they give zero importance to any compliment or positive comments they get. Achieving something is not a reason to celebrate and these people can easily turn something good that should make them feel positive emotions, into something negative, that leads to anxiety, sadness and anger. People who find themselves in this dysfunctional thinking cycle lose the ability to appreciate the simple things in life and eventually that destroys their excitement to live, which can be a huge hazard to their mental health.

An example of Discounting the positives would be if someone was making gradual progress in therapy but couldn't recognize and be happy about it, because the problem still exists nevertheless.

Jumping to conclusions

When a person reaches a conclusion with little to no facts to support it and they suffer before situations even take place. There are two types of "Jumping to Conclusions" thinking patterns:

- **Mind reading**, which is when someone assumes you have a negative opinion about them before you even say anything. It ignores how important communication is to keep healthy relationships and makes people presuppose from the get go that those around them have the worst impression of them.

- **Fortunetelling**, which is when a person predicts that a situation is going to go badly. The person gets nervous and sad before whatever is going to happen even happens.

Going into a situation with the mindset of "This is going to be awful" is halfway to actually messing it up - that is, IF you don't just give up altogether. When you jump to (negative) conclusions you are setting yourself up for failure, ironically because you are afraid you are going to fail, and that messes up with your performance. The reality, as cliché as it may sound, is that you never know if you never try, as that is what people who jump to conclusions need to internalize.

An example of Jumping to Conclusions would be if you assumed the person you are interested in is going to turn you down if you invite them out, so you don't give it a try.

Magnification/Minimization

These two are very common for perfectionists and they happen when a person gives either way too much or not enough importance to situations: usually way too much to negative events and not enough to positive events.

An example of Magnification, also referred to as Catastrophizing, would be if someone thought their relationship was for sure going to end after their first fight with their spouse (instead of focusing on how to work on the problem); and an example of Minimization would be if someone did an amazing job at one of the tasks on their to-do list at work but, in their mind, believed that the day wasn't good, because they didn't have time to finish the second task on the list.

Emotional reasoning

A very prevalent one, that I dare to say you have all felt before. Emotional reasoning is when you believe that just because you feel it, it must be true. It is basically the complete opposite of what CBT stands for. People who have this Cognitive

Distortion don't see the value in factual evidence: all they need is the feeling that things will not go well, and they take that as the truth.

This is a very common thinking pattern for people who suffer from eating disorders: someone with anorexia feels fat, therefore believes they are fat. Even if everyone else around them reassures them that they are not! What they feel is proof enough for it to be considered a fact, which can be a very harmful way of looking at life.

So, an example of Emotional reasoning would simply be "I feel fat, therefore I am fat."

"Should" statements

This Cognitive Distortion is quite self-explanatory. It happens when a person lives in a world of should have, could have, would have; when the thought of "I should..." stops being a source of motivation and starts being a reason of anxiety. This person sets their expectations - of themselves and/or of other - way too high and is always in the mindset of "I should have done this" and "They should have done that." It becomes a very negative cycle:

- For a person's success: they spend so much time thinking about what should happen, that they lose time to actually make it happen.

- For their relationship with others: they expect so much out of their friends, spouse and family members, that they stop appreciating their qualities and good deeds.

This kind of thinking patterns leads to a lot of guilty, unnecessary concerns and disappointment, because the standards that were set (by no one but the person's mind, I should say) were not met.

An example of a "Should" statement is "He should have been a better friend and said yes when I invited him to go out for dinner", after your friend lets you know that they can't go on that date because he already had other plans. In this situation, trying to set the dinner for another date would be a better solution than putting all the attention on the dinner that SHOULD have happened that day.

(Mis)labeling

It happens when someone puts a label on themselves (or others) based on an isolated event. How someone did during that event becomes their biggest characteristic. You did bad? You are bad. You weren't as nice as you could have been? You are a rude person. You didn't eat as healthy as you could have eaten? You are fat. The reality is that most times this label does not even apply, hence the "(Mis)" on (Mis)labeling. It is never positive - or realistic, for that matter - to see a human being as one single (bad) label, whether it is you or someone else, and it prevents you from being able to solve the problem and that is the danger of this Cognitive Distortion. The thought process should be: you did bad? Figure out what you can change to do better next time. You weren't as nice as you could have been? Apologize and make sure you are nice next time. You didn't eat as healthy as you could have eaten? Go to the grocery store and buy only healthy foods, so that you don't have temptations next time.

An example of Labeling is "I failed one test, therefore I am dumb."

Personalization/Blaming

Personalization happens when someone takes everything personally and believes everything bad that happens around them is their fault. Blaming is the exact opposite; it's when someone is incapable of assuming their part of the blame when something goes wrong, and instead puts it all on others. They are both damaging, as you can imagine, for completely different reasons: the person either lives in a state of constant guilt and self-hate, or has no responsibilities in life and is not able to learn with their mistakes.

An example of Personalization would be if a

victim of sexual assault believed the attack was their fault, because of the way they were dressed or of how much alcohol they had consumed; and Blaming would be if the attacker blamed the victim for assault, because of how their outfit or how drunk they were.

These Cognitive Distortions are all quite similar, in the sense that they mess up with your perception of reality and make you see the negative side of a situation, even if that negative side does not exist or is way less important than the positive one. When you find yourself in a Cognitive Distortion thinking cycle, you always see the glass as half empty. As I mentioned before, having this kind of dysfunctional thoughts from time to time is perfectly normal - we all do. But for some people, these distortions become their only way of looking at life and that leads to more serious mental health problems that, fortunately, CBT can help with (some of which I have pointed out above):

Anxiety disorders: defined by Oxford

Medicine as "multiple mental and physiological phenomena, including a person's conscious state of worry over a future unwanted event, or fear of an actual situation"[8]. CBT is a highly recommended practice for anxiety by several General Practitioners, since its success in this kind of situations is evidence based (which is actually not the case for a lot of other types of therapy!). The severity of the anxiety can be low, medium or high, it can be specific to an event or felt generally in the person's daily life and, within anxiety, we can specify some of the most common disorders that are frequently cared for with CBT - phobias, PTSD (Post-Traumatic Stress Disorder), OCD (Obsessive-Compulsive Disorder), social anxiety and panic disorders, for instance; the approach, length and circumstances of the therapy will depend on factors like that.

---

[8] Evans D., Foa, E., Gur R., Hendin H., O'brien C., Seligman M. & Walsh T., (2012). Defining Anxiety Disorders - Oxford Medicine. [online] Available at:
http://oxfordmedicine.com/view/10.1093/9780195173642.001.0001/med-9780195173642-chapter-10 [Accessed 18 Mar. 2019].

The goal of CBT for anxiety is to help the patient comprehend the why of these feelings and learn how to cope with them. To replace the negative with positive and remove the "un" from unrealistic, ultimately improving one's quality of life. To achieve that, the therapist typically goes for two types of CBT techniques: exposure and cognitive restructuring. Exposure (that I explained above, in chapter 4) can be particularly effective to desensitize people with phobias (by facing their fear , OCD and PTSD); while cognitive restructuring, which is the process of rationally thinking about your fears, assessing if they have a reason to be and turning them into positive thoughts, is great for general anxiety disorder and for social anxiety.

Depression: described by the World Health Organization as "a common mental disorder, characterized by persistent sadness and a loss of interest in activities that you normally enjoy, accompanied by an inability to carry out daily activities, for at least two weeks"[9]. CBT is especially advised for people with moderate depression, and it can be used in combination with antidepressants, particularly in cases of more severe depression. The focus in CBT for depression is to help the patient regain their interest in those activities that they used to enjoy and, again, to help them get a rational perspective on their negative thoughts and eventually turn them around.

Eating disorders: defined by the American Psychiatric Association as "illnesses in which the people experience severe disturbances in their eating behaviors and related thoughts and emotions"[10]. CBT can be helpful for any kind of eating disorder, after all, what happens with this kind of condition is that the brain lies to the

---

[9] (2017). WHO | Depression. [online] Available at: https://www.who.int/mental_health/management/depression/en/ [Accessed 19 Mar. 2019].

[10] Parekh, R. (2017). What Are Eating Disorders? [online] Available at: https://www.psychiatry.org/patients-families/eating-disorders/what-are-eating-disorders [Accessed 19 Mar. 2019].

person about their body image and weight, which leads to dangerous actions such as binge eating, purposely starving or self-induce vomiting; and just like for depression, it can be combined with the use of antidepressants. Its effectiveness for bulimia nervosa, however, is the one that stands out.

In fact, when it comes to these illnesses, between the 70s and the 80s, the British psychiatrist Christopher G. Fairburn introduced the concept of CBT-E, which stands for Enhanced Cognitive Behavioral Therapy. You can think of CBT-E as CBT specifically designed for individuals with eating disorders, with techniques that particularly target this kind of mental illness. People who resort to CBT in order to treat their eating disorder are typically suggested exercises that compel them to deconstruct their thinking cycle regarding their shape, weight and eating habits, ultimately making them understand that what they see in the mirror is not the actual truth and how that is damaging their quality of life.

Substance abuse: which is the excessive consumption of a certain substance, whether it is alcohol, any type of drug or tobacco, that gets out of the person's control and has a negative impact on their wellbeing and relationships with others. The approach taken throughout the therapy sessions greatly depends on the patient's willingness and commitment to change their behavior and they can be complemented with other practices, like the attendance of AA meetings for alcohol abusers.

To treat an individual struggling with substance abuse, the therapist typically goes for techniques that will help the patient get a grasp of what personal needs they are fulfilling with the substance they are abusing, which healthier habits they can adopt to continue to fulfill them in the long run and how they can avoid relapses in the future - it is very much about improving their self-awareness and problem-solving skills.

Sexual disorders: defined by the Cleveland Clinic as "a problem occurring during any phase of the sexual response cycle that prevents the individual or couple from experiencing satisfaction from the sexual activity."[11]. These disorders can be anything from problems with ejaculation, lack of interest in sexual activities, pain during sex, female orgasmic disorder and others; and they are usually a consequence of the person's anxiety over their performance in bed, or of physical conditions.

If the reason behind the disorder is of physical nature, it is more effective to go for a treatment that tackles said condition. However, if it is anxiety-related, CBT techniques can be quite helpful, either for an individual or for the couple. The goal when using CBT to treat sexual disorders is to make people put less pressure on themselves and be able to enjoy intimate moments with a partner or by themselves, with a lot of relaxation techniques being involved. When

---

[11] (2015). Sexual Dysfunction & Disorders | Cleveland Clinic. [online] Available at: https://my.clevelandclinic.org/health/diseases/9121-sexual-dysfunction [Accessed 19 Mar. 2019].

both people in the relationship attend the sessions, a lot of communication exercises are also used.

What are NLP's Main Benefits?

You may have noticed in the chapters about NLP that I have used the words success, productivity and efficiency fairly often. This is because the practice can be very beneficent for those looking to take the next step in their career. But, it also works for those struggling with mental health issues.

Psychological Issues

When it comes to mental health problems, the truth is that NLP can be used, but reports of previous experiments have shown mixed results, so I cannot say it is a 100% reliable method. However there are therapists who recur this kind of techniques to alleviate their clients' symptoms, as well as people who have chosen to use NLP to treat their issues and who have had great experiences, so it is an option. Each brain functions in such a different way, that it might just work for you. Whatever is the problem the individual wants to solve, NLP defends the same mindset: that we all have the power to control our mind and, therefore, the way we think and consequently behave. You are not meant to be a victim, but the master of your own life and destiny. So, NLP for psychological issues is all about understanding what leads the person to feel poorly and how they can recompute their thinking process for more positive results. NLP is used to treat these mental problems, among others:

Depression and Anxiety: for someone who goes into an NLP Practitioner office wanting to eliminate their depression and/or anxiety, the therapist would work with the goal of identifying what is causing these mental illnesses, what the person should change to turn the situation around and, of course, some exercises and techniques. It provides the person with efficient weapons to use when those depressive, anxious feelings arise, giving them the power to control their mind and not let it drift away to that bad place, even if it feels strangely comfortable to simply stay there. The Meta Model that I explained in the last chapter for example, is a technique regularly used to fight Depression and Anxiety; as is the recreation of natural bonds, specifically the bond between the mind and the physical body, where NLP for Depression and Anxiety can be even more beneficial when combined with other methods of treatment - like medication and/or the effort to take care of the self - since these conditions can be so intense.

ADHD/ADD: according to the National Institute of Mental Health (NIMH), ADHD/ADD (which stand for Attention-Deficit/Hyperactivity Disorder and Attention Deficit Disorder, respectively) is "a brain disorder marked by an ongoing pattern of inattention and/or hyperactivity-impulsivity that interferes with functioning or development."[12] and it is is very common in children. So, it happens when a person has great difficulty focusing for a long period of time, cannot ever stand still or does not think before saying something or reacting to something. NLP can help people who are struggling with ADHD (even children - I would even say especially with children, since a lot of parents do not like the idea of pumping their kids with pills to control the situation, which is often a solution that is proposed to them. Plus, treating the disorder from the root, and not just by masking the symptoms, from a young age will be very advantageous in the long run, for when the kid turns into an adult) by reprogramming the way they process information.

That is, right now the person with ADHD does not have any control over their thinking

---

[12] (n.d.). NIMH >> Attention-Deficit/Hyperactivity Disorder. [online] Available at: https://www.nimh.nih.gov/health/topics/attention-deficit-hyperactivity-disorder-adhd/index.shtml [Accessed 18 Mar. 2019].

processes, everything happens way too fast and that shows in the way they behave, which can be very overwhelming. Changing that will take practice, but with exercises that help them train the task of staying focused on one unique thing, ultimately the person will improve their concentration skills. The attention disorder can also be the result of a traumatic event, in which case NLP will go back to such event and help the client figure out how they can change the way they look at it, to put it in a more positive light and stop it from causing learning difficulties. If you take your child to NLP sessions to treat ADHD/ADD, we suggest you join them because it will be important for you to know how you can give them support in situations where the disorder gets more severe (but, of course, you should follow your child's coach's instructions regarding your presence).

Borderline Personality Disorder: this disorder is defined by NIMH as "a mental illness marked by an ongoing pattern of varying moods, self-image, and behavior. These symptoms often result in impulsive actions and problems in relationships. People with borderline personality disorder may experience intense episodes of anger, depression, and anxiety that can last from a few hours to days."[13]. So for someone with Borderline Personality Disorder, their thinking patterns are so incongruent that they lose themselves in the middle of several different opinions, moods, mindsets and reality maps. They do not have a real sense of self, but they feel like anyone who disagrees with them is their enemy. Feeling this way can result in self-hate and self-destructive behaviors, as well as damage in the relationships with others. Through NLP, someone who suffers from this disorder understands what they are mismatching that leads them to have this personality incongruency and what they can do to match it and find their

---

[13] (2017). NIMH >> Borderline Personality Disorder. [online] Available at:
https://www.nimh.nih.gov/health/topics/borderline-personality-disorder/index.shtml [Accessed 19 Mar. 2019].

true sense of self. During the entire process of working with a person with Borderline Personality Disorder, it is crucial that the NLP Practitioner puts effort into building a rapport with their client and that they always make sure that they are safe, since this disorder can make people dangerous, due to the fact that they can react negatively to different opinions and points of view.

OCD: Obsessive-Compulsive Disorders are a type of anxiety, as was mentioned before, and the way NLP can help overcome it is by understanding the cycle and breaking it. The Anchoring technique can be quite effective to help with OCD, since it teaches the person to go from one negative feeling (the anxiety) to a positive one (relaxation), by repeatedly using an anchor (whichever trigger the person chooses). NLP will help someone with OCD have more realistic trains of thought, instead of obsessing over something to the point that it causes them to freak out about something that is perfectly fine.

Performance at Work

If you had heard of NLP before you started reading this ebook, there is a strong likelihood that you have seen it being associated with career-related issues. And indeed, practicing NLP is considered to be a great way of giving professionals the push they need to take the next step in their career. This practice can be useful for everyone in the hierarchy of a company, because everyone, no matter which stage of the career they are in, has space to grow and skills to perfect.

However, NLP is more commonly practiced by people in roles of authority, such as team leaders, CEOs and teachers. That makes sense, when you think about the fact that your success as a leader depends greatly on how well you can understand, relate to and communicate with others. In other words, in how good your skills of building a rapport and using it to productively communicate are. NLP can teach the professional how to see their own mistakes, as well as their team's, as learning opportunities (and as something that will always happen and that is perfectly normal), how to understand and keep in mind the emotions of their team members, how to remain calm in situations of high pressure and how to be continuously encouraging to the team. The same applies to a teacher and their relationship with the students. Don't those sound like amazing traits for your boss or your teacher to have?

In fact, there are really powerful people in the world who have resourced to NLP in order to improve their overall leading and communication skills, and who swear by it, such as Barack Obama and Oprah (who even has several pages of her websites dedicated to this practice). Take Barack Obama's example, who has used countless NLP techniques in his speeches and public appearances. A very common one is he would repeatedly tell the audience something that Americans as a nation believed in (for instance, how the economy was in a bad state), to then say what he was going to do as the President and install in their minds the connection between "Barack Obama" and "change for the better" and use that as the reason as to why he should be elected.

But if you are not in a position of authority at your workplace, don't just assume NLP cannot be for you. Practicing NLP can be a great tool to better understand your boss and, as a result, better communicate with them and get a better grasp of what they expect from your performance. Knowing this allows you to make more efficient work plans, since you can cross your career goals and your boss's expectations and make everyone involved happy. Plus, when you are on the same page as your boss, not only will they probably notice it, but it will prevent conflicts between the two of you. All of this offers you great advantages at work and better chances of going up in the hierarchy, if that is your goal.

There is also the possibility that you do work, but not for a company, for example if you are a freelancer or a solo entrepreneur. If this is your case, NLP is also for you. Working by yourself involves a lot - and I mean a lot - of networking. You need clients, you need to make your name known, you may need to partner up with other companies and professionals to make your business work. Doing all of this becomes a lot easier if your communication skills are perfected to their very best, which is something you can achieve with sessions of NLP Coaching.

Whether you are a team leader, a freelancer or a manager, there are two industries where the benefits of practicing NLP stand out: Sales and Human Resources/Talent Spotting. A good salesperson needs to be a good communicator; in that industry, there is no other option. They need to know how to persuade, they need to be self-confident and they need to know how to build rapport with just about anyone. In order to sell, the person should be able to meet the (hopefully future) customer in their thinking process, to know how they can influence them and turn a no into a yes, in case there is some resistance at first. When it comes to HR and Talent Spotters, professionals spend their daily life dealing with people. They analyze profiles, they are the direct contact for people who apply for jobs or who are chosen to be recruited, they manage the entire recruiting process and they are the bridge between the employees and the employers. This requires them to have excellent communication and problem-solving skills, as well as the ability to spot and attract the best talent possible. Besides all of this, in both industries the professionals need to be focused on success and keep a positive mindset. As you have read throughout this book, these are all skills NLP can help individuals with, which is why it is so relevant for the two professional fields.

Chapter 5: CBT vs. NLP

So now you are familiar with both concepts: you know what they are based on, how they were introduced, how you can practice them, what they are good for and even some exercises you can try. But alas, this is a contrast and compare ebook, so in this chapter I will summarize the main differences and similarities between Cognitive Behavioral Therapy and Neuro-Linguistic Programming, in order to make it easier for you to assess which one you should choose for yourself.

The Main Differences Between CBT and NLP

Problem-Oriented vs. Growth-Oriented

For starters, the two models differ in what kind of issues they tackle in terms of when they happen. CBT is usually used to solve specific problems: you go into the therapist's office, you let them know what you are struggling with and, as a duo, you work on that specific issue. CBT is problem-oriented. Then, you are expected to apply what you learn in therapy in real-life negative situations and, as you get different outcomes (more positive than you were expecting), you consciously start to change your mindset and eliminate dysfunctional thinking patterns. When it comes to NPL, the practice is not as specific; instead it is typically used for the client to take the next step in their journey, to learn unconscious techniques they can continuously apply to their life in order to grow as their own person and/or as a professional: NLP is growth-oriented.

Conscious vs. Unconscious

The two practices focus on different parts of the brain to help their clients reach their goals and some would say this is the biggest difference between them. CBT teaches people how to consciously change their dysfunctional thinking patterns, with sessions that almost feel like classes and with regular homework; on the other hand; NLP makes people aware of their conscious mind, but more importantly, teaches them how to reach their unconscious and change their thinking patterns and internal representations in that level, with techniques that are commonly compared to hypnosis, which means that harmful thoughts are treated from their root. So in CBT, the therapist tells the person what the nasty consequences of their thoughts are, while in NLP the Practitioner makes the people live those consequences, through those hypnotic NLP practices. This means that someone who chooses CBT learns ways of purposely turning a moment of struggle around, while someone who recurs to NLP ends the training with coping mechanisms that automatically activate in such type of moment. So, in NLP, change is produced at a deeper level than in CBT.

High Need for Individual's Input vs. Low Need for Individual's Input

I mentioned right at the beginning of this book

that CBT is a talking therapy, so as you can imagine, it is the one between these two that needs the client to constantly share their input, what they are feeling, the progress they make and difficulties they are faced with along the way and any other information the therapist (or the client) finds relevant to increase the chances of success as much as possible. Contrarily, for an NLP Coach, there is no need for the client to dig into their problems and go into details, all the Practitioner needs is for the individual to share just enough for them to be able to help. NLP is content independent.

The Main Similarities Between CBT and NLP

Focus on Changing Dysfunctional Thinking Patterns

The end goal for both practices is the same: to identify dysfunctional, harmful and limiting trains of thought the client constantly has and turn them into realistic, beneficial and more ecological ones. They make the client aware of irrational, unrealistic interpretations of the world, of themselves, of other people and of specific events, that lead them to risky states of mind and behaviors, as well as of how they can overcome them. The importance of keeping a positive mindset is clear for both, as well as the idea that we can have control over our brains, if we just practice.

Focus on Perception of Events Instead of the Actual Events

For both CBT and NLP, you build your own reality. The event that happens is not important: what matters and what should be taken into account is the way you interpret said event. Just think about it, both practices work towards changing the individual's thinking patterns. If the focus was on the actual events, this kind of approach would never work.

Focus on the Present and not the Past

What matters is right now. Although, if you attend sessions of CBT or NLP you will be asked about your past, that will not be the focus for either of the practices. Your current thinking patterns and maps of reality and the current consequences of those in your life: that is what these practices will work with. And what you will learn is how to deal with the present: techniques and practical exercises that help alleviate the problems you have now and to improve your current state of mind, and not how you can deal or be at peace with the things that happened in your past that may have lead you to where you are now, mentally.

Putting the Responsibility on the Individual

For both CBT and NLP, the person's commitment and willingness to put in their effort is absolutely crucial. The therapist/coach is no more than a guide for the process but the work depends on the person. Someone who is not ready to take responsibility for their dysfunctional thinking patterns and to actively work on them, is not ready for either of the practices discussed in this ebook. As you may have understood in the

Chapter that talks about some examples of techniques, both models are very practical, unlike some other types of therapy where maybe the client only has to talk during that specific amount of time (which works greatly for some people, of course). For these two, you have to want to do it in order to make it work.

CBT or NLP: Which One is Right For You?

Figuring out which one of the two you should choose might be tricky, but my advice would be that you focus your decision on your end goal and on what kind of problem you are trying to treat. If have you read this entire ebook, you have a better idea of what kind of issues Cognitive Behavioral Therapy and what Neuro-Linguistic Programming can successfully tackle and you may have even made a choice already. But, in case you are still on the fence about which one would be more effective in your specific situation, reflect on the following questions:

What do you want help with?

- A. Your mental health;
- B. Issues related to your professional life.

Do you have time to do homework (that you will constantly be asked about in your sessions)?

- A. Yes and I am willing to put effort into doing this homework as best as I can;
- B. No, I am too busy to have homework on top of all my other tasks. However I am willing to practice every time I have free time to do so.

Do you feel comfortable opening up and talking about what is haunting you?

- A. Yes, I am ready to be an open book to my therapist and give them all the information they find relevant and that I am ready to (knowing that I will never be forced to do it);
- B. No, I would prefer an approach were

my continuous input is not necessary.

Is the issue I am trying to solve:

- A. Specific and easy to define?
- B. Or general (such as general nervousness or an overall communication problem)?

Are you looking for:

- A. A more logical approach, where you can clearly know step by step how you tackle your problem and turn it around?
- B. Or an approach that is not as objective, where you do not need to know each step, but that will implement the changes in yourself subconsciously, ultimately making those changes automatically happen when you are faced with a trigger?

Are you looking to:

A. Find solutions for yourself?

B. Or learn to the point where eventually you will be ready to help others with their own issues?

Is your end goal to:

A. Solve a problem and move on?

B. Explore your potential and grow as a person or as a professional?

If your answers were mostly A, I would suggest you try Cognitive Behavioral Therapy. If, on the other hand, you choose mostly the B options, consider giving Neuro-Linguistic Programming a try.

Some other aspects to have in mind when choosing:

- If your goal is to deal with a problem from your past, to get answers about it and come to terms with it, like an abusive childhood, for example, neither of the practices is right for you.

- You can look for real-life testimonies of people who were in a similar situation to yours and who underwent these therapies, either from people you know personally or by looking for reviews online. Everyone's experience is different but talking to people who have been there will always give more insights that you can consider when it is time to choose.

- You can always try one and, if it does not work, you can give the other one a chance. This is actually quite a common thing to do and if you have done some research online, I am sure you came across cases like that.

- The therapist you choose has a big influence on how effective the therapy is. So, if the first one you go for doesn't seem to be right for you, try to understand if your relationship with the therapist is good and if they fulfill the requirements I mentioned in both "What to Look For In a CBT Therapist/NLP Coach?" subchapters. It is critical that you keep this in mind, so that you don't miss the opportunity of finding the right therapy for you based on one bad experience.

- If you want to treat mental health issues, CBT and NLP can actually be complementary, so you can enroll in an NLP training while also attending CBT sessions and get benefits from both practices (do not forget, however, to let your CBT therapist know that you are trying NLP as well, as it is probably important information for them to know).

Conclusion

CBT is not better than NLP and NLP is not better than CBT. They work for some people and don't work for others, because as has been mentioned throughout the book, each brain works differently, we all have different issues we are struggling with and we all go to therapy with different end goals. By now, you know a lot more information about CBT and NLP, so when it is time for you to choose one of them, look at the whole picture and consider all the aspects I mentioned above: related to you, related to the therapy itself and related to the therapist.

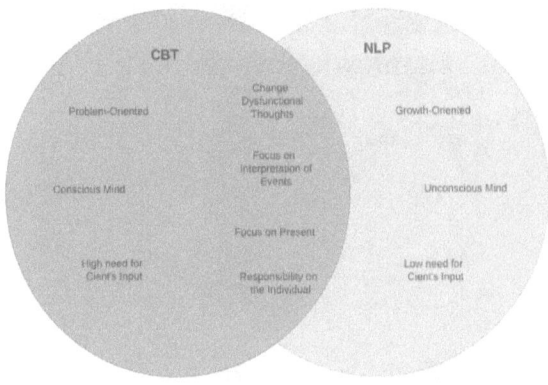

If you are struggling with mental health problems, do not hesitate to get help. Talk to your loved ones if you need support. Besides that, with one quick Google search you can find the mental health helplines in your area, so if you are ever in a moment of extreme struggle, contact them, as they will know how to calm you down and pull you out of that darkness. And don't forget: with the right support system, everything gets better and you will realize that there is so much to live for. The time for you to start feeling better is now!

Please don't forget to leave a positive review of this ebook. Thank you for reading and I wish you the best of luck!

References

Ackerman, C. (2017). Cognitive Behavioral Therapy | Psychology Today. [online] Psychology Today. Available at: https://www.psychologytoday.com/us/basics/cognitive-behavioral-therapy [Accessed 16 Mar. 2019].

Anxiety Canada. (n.d.). More on CBT. [online] Available at: https://www.anxietycanada.com/help-resources/cbt/more-on-cbt [Accessed 16 Mar. 2019].

appendix2.2. (n.d.). [ebook] Available at: http://supp.apa.org/books/Making-Evidence-Based-Psychological-Treatments-Work-With-Older-Adults/appendix2.2.pdf [Accessed 16 Mar. 2019].

Brainmass.com. (2018). [online] Available at: https://brainmass.com/psychology/abnormal-psychology/counselling-psychology-comparing-ellis-vs-beck-133832 [Accessed 16 Mar. 2019].

Cambridgecognition.com. (n.d.). What Is Cognition & Cognitive Behaviour - Cambridge Cognition. [online] Available at: https://www.cambridgecognition.com/blog/entry/what-is-cognition [Accessed 16 Mar. 2019].

CBT_april2010. (n.d.). [PDF] Available at: https://www.integration.samhsa.gov/clinical-practice/sbirt/cbt_overview_part_1.pdf [Accessed 16 Mar. 2019].

First CBT appointment - prompt. (n.d.). [PDF] Available at: https://www.get.gg/docs/FirstApptPrompt.pdf [Accessed 16 Mar. 2019].

Habitsforwellbeing.com. (n.d.). Cognitive Behaviour Therapy (ABC Model). [online] Available at: https://www.habitsforwellbeing.com/cognitive-behaviour-therapy-abc-model/ [Accessed 16 Mar. 2019].

Hall, G. (2018). [online] Timewith.co.uk. Available at: https://timewith.co.uk/blog/what-to-expect-in-your-first-cbt-session [Accessed 16 Mar. 2019].

Leigh, J. (2018). What to expect in your first CBT session. [online] Jessica Leigh CBT. Available at: http://www.jessicaleighcbt.com/blog/2018/1/10/what-to-expect-in-your-first-cbt-session [Accessed 16 Mar. 2019].

Mcleod, S. (n.d.). Cognitive Behavioral Therapy | CBT | Simply Psychology. [online] Simplypsychology.org. Available at: https://www.simplypsychology.org/cognitive-therapy.html [Accessed 16 Mar. 2019].

Nami.org. (n.d.). Psychotherapy | NAMI: National Alliance on Mental Illness. [online] Available at: https://www.nami.org/Learn-More/Treatment/Psychotherapy [Accessed 16 Mar. 2019].

nhs.uk. (n.d.). How it works. [online] Available at: https://www.nhs.uk/conditions/cognitive-behavioural-therapy-cbt/how-it-works/ [Accessed 16 Mar. 2019].

Study.com. (n.d.). Behavior: Definition & Explanation - Video & Lesson Transcript | Study.com. [online] Available at: https://study.com/academy/lesson/behavior-definition-lesson-quiz.html [Accessed 16 Mar. 2019].

Willard, E. (n.d.). Explaining Depression - Beck's Cognitive Triad | tutor2u Psychology. [online] tutor2u. Available at: https://www.tutor2u.net/psychology/reference/explaining-depression-becks-cognitive-triad [Accessed 16 Mar. 2019].

Cogbtherapy.com. (n.d.). What to Expect in CBT - Cognitive Behavioral Therapy Los Angeles. [online] Available at: http://cogbtherapy.com/what-happens-in-cbt [Accessed 16 Mar. 2019].

Gillihan, S. (2016). Therapy Without a Therapist? | Psychology Today. [online] Available at:

https://www.psychologytoday.com/us/blog/think-act-be/201609/therapy-without-therapist [Accessed 16 Mar. 2019].

Anxietycanada.com. (n.d.). Calm Breathing | Anxiety Canada. [online] Available at: https://www.psychologytoday.com/us/blog/think-act-be/201609/therapy-without-therapist [Accessed 16 Mar. 2019].

Walkalong.ca. (n.d.). Realistic Thinking | Walk Along. [online] Available at: https://www.walkalong.ca/RealisticThinking [Accessed 16 Mar. 2019].

Anxietycanada.com. (n.d.). Helpful Thinking | Anxiety Canada. [online] Available at: https://www.anxietycanada.com/adults/helpful-thinking [Accessed 16 Mar. 2019].

Riebe G., Fan M., Unützer J., Vannoy S. (2012). Activity Scheduling as a Core Component of Effective Care Management for Late-Life Depression. [online] Available at: https://www.ncbi.nlm.nih.gov/pmc/articles/PM

C3429703/ [Accessed 16 Mar. 2019].

Anxietycanada.com. (n.d.). How to do Progressive Muscle Relaxation. [PDF] Available at: https://www.anxietycanada.com/sites/default/files/MuscleRelaxation.pdf [Accessed 16 Mar. 2019].

Joaquin. (2018). Progressive Muscle Relaxation (PMR): A Positive Psychology Guide. [online] Available at: https://positivepsychologyprogram.com/progressive-muscle-relaxation-pmr/ [Accessed 16 Mar. 2019].

Cci.health.wa.gov. (n.d.). Progressive Muscle Relaxation. [PDF] Available at: https://www.cci.health.wa.gov.au/~/media/CCI/Mental%20Health%20Professionals/Panic/Panic%20-%20Information%20Sheets/Panic%20Information%20Sheet%20-%2005%20-%20Progressive%20Muscle%20Relaxation.pdf

[Accessed 16 Mar. 2019].

Healthywa.wa.gov.au. (n.d.). Progressive muscle relaxation. [online] Available at: https://healthywa.wa.gov.au/Articles/N_R/Progressive-muscle-relaxation [Accessed 17 Mar. 2019].

Anxietytreatmentexperts.com. (n.d.). Cognitive Behavioral Therapy and Exposure and Response Prevention Therapy. [online] Available at: http://anxietytreatmentexperts.com/cbt-exposure-response-prevention-therapy/ [Accessed 18 Mar. 2019].

Cogbtherapy.com. (n.d.). Exposure Therapy. [online] Available at: http://cogbtherapy.com/exposure-therapy-los-angeles [Accessed 18 Mar. 2019].

Goodtherapy.org. (n.d.). Exposure Therapy. [online] Available at: https://www.goodtherapy.org/learn-about-therapy/types/exposure-therapy [Accessed 18 Mar. 2019].

Div12.org. (n.d.). Microsoft Word - what is exposure therapy.doc. [PDF] Available at: https://www.div12.org/sites/default/files/WhatIsExposureTherapy.pdf [Accessed 18 Mar. 2019].

Borchard, T. (n.d.). 10 Cognitive Distortions. [online] Available at: https://www.everydayhealth.com/columns/therese-borchard-sanity-break/10-cognitive-distortions/ [Accessed 18 Mar. 2019].

Gattuso, R. (2018). 5 Ways Black and White Thinking Positions Your Perspective. [online] Available at: https://www.talkspace.com/blog/black-white-thinking-ways-poisons-your-perspective/ [Accessed 18 Mar. 2019].

Cogbtherapy.com. (2015). Cognitive Distortions: Overgeneralizing. [online] Available at: http://cogbtherapy.com/cbt-blog/cognitive-distortions-overgeneralizing [Accessed 18 Mar. 2019].

Thompson, M. (2017). Cognitive Distortions:

Mental Filter - Wild Therapy Psychotherapy. [online] Available at: https://wildtreewellness.com/mental/ [Accessed 18 Mar. 2019].

Kos, B. (n.d.). Fortunetelling, mind reading and jumping to conclusions. [online] Available at: https://agileleanlife.com/jumping-to-conclusions/ [Accessed 18 Mar. 2019].

Star, K. (2019). Cognitive Distortions: Magnification and Minimization. [online] Available at: https://www.verywellmind.com/magnification-and-minimization-2584183 [Accessed 18 Mar. 2019].

Seltzer, L. (2017). What's "Emotional Reasoning"—And Why Is It Such a Problem? [online] Available at: https://www.psychologytoday.com/us/blog/evolution-the-self/201706/what-s-emotional-reasoning-and-why-is-it-such-problem [Accessed 18 Mar.2019].

Star, K. (2018). How Should Statements Contribute to Panic and Anxiety. [online] Available at: https://www.verywellmind.com/should-statements-2584193 [Accessed 18 Mar. 2019].

Cogbtherapy.com. (2015). Cognitive Distortions: Labeling. [online] Available at: http://cogbtherapy.com/cbt-blog/cognitive-distortions-labeling [Accessed 18 Mar. 2019].

Oxfordmedicine.com. (2012). Defining Anxiety Disorders - Oxford Medicine. [online] Available at: http://oxfordmedicine.com/view/10.1093/9780195173642.001.0001/med-9780195173642-chapter-10 [Accessed 18 Mar. 2019].

Klearminds.com. (2014). How Cognitive Behavioural Therapy Can Help Treat Anxiety Disorders. [online] Available at: https://www.klearminds.com/blog/cognitive-behavioural-therapy-can-help-treat-anxiety-disorders/ [Accessed 18 Mar. 2019].

Kaczkurkin, A., Foa, E. (2015). Cognitive-behavioral therapy for anxiety disorders: an update on the empirical evidence. [online] Available at: https://www.ncbi.nlm.nih.gov/pmc/articles/PMC4610618/ [Accessed 18 Mar. 2019].

Cuncic, A. (2019). Cognitive-Behavioral Therapy Use for Social Media Anxiety. [online] Available at: https://www.verywellmind.com/how-is-cbt-used-to-treat-sad-3024945 [Accessed 18 Mar. 2019].

Gonzalez, K. (n.d.). Cognitive Behavioral Therapy Techniques for Anxiety | Study.com. [online] Available at: https://study.com/academy/lesson/cognitive-behavioral-therapy-techniques-for-anxiety.html [Accessed 18 Mar. 2019].

Webmd.com. (n.d.). Cognitive Behavioral Therapy (CBT) for Negative Thinking & Depression. [online] Available at: https://www.webmd.com/depression/guide/cog

nitive-behavioral-therapy-for-depression#2
[Accessed 18 Mar. 2019].

Beckinstitute.org. (n.d.). Depression | Beck Institute for Cognitive Behavior Therapy. [online] Available at: https://beckinstitute.org/detail/depression/ [Accessed 18 Mar. 2019].

Holland, K. (2016). Cognitive Behavioral Therapy for Depression. [online] Available at: https://www.healthline.com/health/depression/cognitive-behavioral-therapy [Accessed 18 Mar. 2019].

Psychiatry.org. (n.d.). What Are Eating Disorders? [online] Available at: https://www.psychiatry.org/patients-families/eating-disorders/what-are-eating-disorders [Accessed 18 Mar. 2019].

Bodywhys.is. (n.d.). Bodywhys | Understanding CBT-E: Cognitive Behavioral Therapy-Enhanced. [online] Available at: https://www.bodywhys.ie/treatment-pathway/cbt-e-cognitive-behavioural-therapy-enhanced/ [Accessed 18 Mar. 2019].

Beckinstitute.org. (2016). Treating Substance Misuse Disorders with CBT | Beck Institute for Cognitive Behavioral Therapy. [online] Available at: https://beckinstitute.org/treating-substance-misuse-disorders-cbt/ [Accessed 18 Mar. 2019].

Clevelandclinic.org. (n.d.). Sexual Dysfunction & Disorders | Cleveland Clinic. [online] Available at: https://my.clevelandclinic.org/health/diseases/9121-sexual-dysfunction [Accessed 18 Mar. 2019].

Beckinstitute.org. (n.d.). Sexual Dysfunctions | Beck Institute for Cognitive Behavioral Therapy. [online] Available at: https://beckinstitute.org/detail/sexual-dysfunctions/ [Accessed 18 Mar. 2019].

Nlp.com. (n.d.). What is NLP? [online] Available at: http://www.nlp.com/what-is-nlp/ [Accessed 18 Mar. 2019].

Lowther, D. (2012). Introducing Neurolinguistic Programming (NLP) for Work. [ebook] Available at: https://books.google.pt/books?id=5AlnAgAAQBAJ&pg=PT13&lpg=PT13&dq=nlp+first+access&source=bl&ots=ty1o4K0Uyx&sig=ACfU3U1YtixmDDJ0yjbKR1VztWSpU-rS4w&hl=en&sa=X&ved=2ahUKEwi6oZH_yu7gAhUSgHMKHX3OCMkQ6AEwFH0ECAEQAQ#v=onepage&q&f=false [Accessed 18 Mar. 2019].

Elston, T. (n.d.). NLP Training: The Basics - NLP World. [online] Available at: https://www.nlpworld.co.uk/nlp-training-the-basics/ [Accessed 18 Mar. 2019].

Bayareaocd.com. (n.d.). Choosing a CBT Therapist | Bay Area OCD and Anxiety Center. [online] Available at: https://bayareaocd.com/choosing-a-cbt-therapist [Accessed 18 Mar. 2019].

Simon, G. (2016). Effective Therapist Qualities and CBT. [online] Available at:

https://counsellingresource.com/features/2016/10/03/effective-therapist-qualities/ [Accessed 18 Mar. 2019].

Puceliknlp.com. (n.d.). Frank Pucelik. [online] Available at: http://puceliknlp.com/#rec18089120 [Accessed 18 Mar. 2019].

Chrismorris.com. (n.d.). Frank Pucelik and the early days of NLP - Chris Morris Online. [online] Available at: http://www.chrismorris.com/blog/2010/09/frank-pucelik-and-the-early-days-of-nlp/ [Accessed 18 Mar. 2019].

Hedley, J. (2016) The history of NLP, part 3: The Gestalt Base of NLP. [online] Available at: https://www.thecoachingroom.com.au/blog/the-history-of-nlp-part-3-the-gestalt-base-of-nlp [Accessed 18 Mar. 2019].

Crownhouse.co.uk. (n.d.). The Origins of Neuro Linguistic Programming. [online] Available at: https://www.crownhouse.co.uk/publications/the

-origins-of-neuro-linguistic-programming [Accessed 18 Mar. 2019].

Cattelan, L. (n.d.). NLP Model of Communication --4 Pillars to Getting Desired Results. [online] Available at: https://www.selfgrowth.com/articles/nlp_model_of_communication4_pillars_to_getting_desired_results [Accessed 18 Mar. 2019].

Dieck, W. (2017). Four Pillars of Neuro-Linguistic Programming - Hypnosis San Diego | Hypnotherapist | NLP Total Mind TherapyHypnosis San Diego | Hypnotherapist | NLP Total Mind Therapy. [online] Available at: http://www.totalmindtherapy.net/neuro-linguistic-programming/four-pillars-of-neuro-linguistic-programming/ [Accessed 18 Mar. 2019].

White, J. (2016). The Four Pillars Of NLP - John White - Medium. [online] Available at: https://medium.com/@john.white.jw336/the-four-pillars-of-nlp-b566154b7a70 [Accessed 18

Mar. 2019].

Hubs, M. (2013). Self-Help & Applied Psychology: The Four Pillars of NLP (Neuro Linguistic Programming) | HubPages. [online] Available at: https://hubpages.com/education/The-Four-Pillars-Of-NLP-Neuro-Linguistic-Programming-Outcomes-Sensory-Acuity-Behavioural-Flexibility-Rapport [Accessed 18 Mar. 2019].

Lim, J. (2014). The Four-Pillar Formula Towards Any Success | Jacky Lim. [online] Available at: http://www.jackylim.com/blog/four-pillar-formula-towards-success [Accessed 18 Mar. 2019].

Skillsyouneed.com. (n.d.). Dilts' Logical Levels | SkillsYouNeed. [online] Available at: https://www.skillsyouneed.com/lead/logical-levels.html [Accessed 18 Mar. 2019].

Nlp-now.co.uk. (m.d.). The NLP Logical Levels - Pegasus NLP. [online] Available at: https://nlp-now.co.uk/nlp-logical-levels/?doing_wp_cron=1552926922.7531158924102783203125 [Accessed 18 Mar. 2019].

Metcalf, D.& Njoroge, D. (2008). Neuro Linguistic Programming (NLP). [online] Available at: http://www.cimaglobal.com/Documents/ImportedDocuments/cid_tg_neuro_linguistic_programming_jan08.pdf.pdf [Accessed 18 Mar. 2019].

Elston, T. (n.d.). NLP Practitioner - Presuppositions of NLP - NLP World. [online] Available at: https://www.nlpworld.co.uk/nlp-presuppositions/ [Accessed 18 Mar. 2019].

Mindacademy.com. (n.d.). NLP Vooronderstellingen | Model van da wereld. [online] Available at: http://www.mindacademy.com/nlp/presuppositions-of-nlp [Accessed 18 Mar. 2019].

Nlpfasttrack.com. (n.d.). NLP Presupposition - The Meaning of Communication is the response you get - Anergy NLP Singapore & Hong Kong. [online] Available at:

http://www.nlpfasttrack.com/nlp-presupposition-the-meaning-of-communication-is-the-response-you-get/ [Accessed 18 Mar. 2019].

Mymotivational-nlp.com. (n.d.). A person is not his or her behaviour. [online] Available at: http://www.mymotivational-nlp.com/nlp-presuppositions/1-a-person-is-not-his-or-her-behaviour [Accessed 18 Mar. 2019].

Hoag, J. (n.d.). NLP Presupposition: The Map is Not the Territory, by John David Hoag. [online] Available at: http://www.nlpls.com/articles/mapTerritory.php [Accessed 18 Mar. 2019].

Joah, J. (n.d.). NLP Presupposition: Positive Intention, by John David Hoag. [online] Available at: http://www.nlpls.com/articles/positiveIntent.php [Accessed 18 Mar. 2019].

Craig. (2017). NLP Presuppositions | Grass Roots NLP. [online] Available at:

https://grassrootsnlp.com/nlp-presuppositions [Accessed 18 Mar. 2019].

Nlppod.com. (n.d.). NLP Presuppositions (7): I am in charge of my mind, and therefore my results - Practical NLP Podcast. [online] Available at: https://nlppod.com/nlp-presuppositions-7-i-am-in-charge-of-my-mind-and-therefore-my-results/ [Accessed 18 Mar. 2019].

Dangeli, J. (n.d.). The Presuppositions of NLP | Jevon Dangeli.com. [online] Available at: https://jevondangeli.com/the-presuppositions-of-nlp-2/ [Accessed 18 Mar. 2019].

Mymotivational-nlp.com. (n.d.). Having choice is better than not having choice. [online] Available at: http://www.mymotivational-nlp.com/nlp-presuppositions/5-having-choice-is-better-than-not-having-choice [Accessed 18 Mar. 2019].

Anlp.org. (n.d.). Wyatt Woodsmall - NLP - Neuro Linguistic Programming. [online] Available at:

https://anlp.org/wyatt-woodsmall [Accessed 18 Mar. 2019].

Elston, T. (n.d.). NLP Training - The Human Communication Model - NLP World. [online] Available at: https://www.nlpworld.co.uk/thehumancommunicationmodel-blog/ [Accessed 18 Mar. 2019].

Schneider, J. (n.d.). The NLP Model of Perception | Perception Academy NLP Training, Neuro-Semantics and Life Coach. [online] Available at: https://perceptionacademy.com/the-nlp-communication-model/ [Accessed 18 Mar. 2019].

Atmabhan.com. (n.d.). NLP Communication Model.pdf. [PDF] Available at: http://atmabhan.com/Mumbai/pdf/NLP%20Communication%20Model.pdf [Accessed 18 Mar. 2019].

Benalbertscomapny.co.za. (n.d.). Whats is NLP? How can it help me [online] Available at: http://www.benalbertscompany.co.za/about_nlp

/ [Accessed 18 Mar. 2019].

Dangeli, J. (n.d.). The NLP Communication Model | Jevon Dangeli.com. [online] Available at: https://jevondangeli.com/the-nlp-communication-model/ [Accessed 18 Mar. 2019].

Microdot.net. (n.d.). NLP Communication Model. [online] Available at: http://www.microdot.net/nlp/learning-strategy/communication-model.shtml [Accessed 18 Mar. 2019].

Booher, M. (n.d.). NLP communication model. [online] Available at: http://www.professionalinfluence.com/reading-your-customer/176-nlp-communication-model [Accessed 18 Mar. 2019].

Alchemyassistant.com. (n.d.). Deletions, distortions and generalisations. [online] Available at: https://www.alchemyassistant.com/topics/VKSWRiWxcLWMhBrf.html [Accessed 18 Mar. 2019].

Nlpreno.com. (n.d.). NLP Communication Model Part 2 - NLP RENO. [online] Available at: https://www.nlpreno.com/nlp-communication-model [Accessed 18 Mar. 2019].

Cult.bg. (2018). NLP (Neuro Linguistic Programming) Getting Started With Courses. [online] Available at: https://cult.bg/nlp-getting-started/ [Accessed 18 Mar. 2019].

Apps, J. (2005). Microsoft Word - A Guide to Choosing an NLP Practitioner Course 1 2-09.doc. [PDF] Available at: https://anlp.org/files/pdf-guide-to-choosing-an-nlp-practitioner-course_31_132.pdf [Accessed 18 Mar. 2019].

Scribd.com. (n.d.). How Do You Structure and NLP Therapy Session | Neuro Linguistic Programming | Feeling. [online] Available at: https://www.scribd.com/document/29057235/How-Do-You-Structure-and-NLP-Therapy-Session [Accessed 18 Mar. 2019].

Cave, P. (n.d.). What happens in a typical session | master hypnotherapy and neuro linguistic programming practitioner training. [online] Available at: https://patrickcave.com/therapy/what-happens-in-a-session/ [Accessed 18 Mar. 2019].

Hoobyar, T. (2010) Hot To Do NLP On Yourself - NLP Comprehensive. [online] Available at: https://www.nlpco.com/how-to-do-nlp-on-yourself/ [Accessed 18 Mar. 2019].

Nlpnotes.com. (n.d.). Presuppositions: Lost Performative - NLP NotesNLP Notes. [online] Available at: http://nlpnotes.com/presuppositions-lost-performative/ [Accessed 18 Mar. 2019].

Nlp-mentor.com. (n.d.). Simple deletions. [online] Available at: https://nlp-mentor.com/simple-deletions/ [Accessed 18 Mar. 2019].

O'Brien, D. (2009). Reserve Meta Model: Simple Deletions - Ericksonian. [online] Available at: http://ericksonian.com/reverse-meta-model-simple-deletions [Accessed 18 Mar. 2019].

Avery, L. (2015). Meta-Model Distinctions - Deletions | NLP4UOnline. [online] Available at: http://nlp4uonline.com/blog/2015/05/15/meta-model-distinctions-deletions/ [Accessed 18 Mar. 2019].

Hoag, J. (n.d.). NLP Meta Model, by John David Hoag. [online] Available at: http://www.nlpls.com/articles/NLPmetaModel.php [Accessed 18 Mar. 2019].

Elston, T. (n.d.). NLP World - NLP Training - Meta Model. [online] Available at: https://www.nlpworld.co.uk/nlp-training-meta-model/ [Accessed 18 Mar. 2019].

Quizlet.com. (n.d.). Meta Model Violations - Examples Flashcards | Quizlet [online] Available at: https://quizlet.com/64459572/meta-model-violations-examples-flash-cards/ [Accessed 18 Mar. 2019].

Nlpworld.co.uk. (n.d.). NLP Nominalization | NLP World - Glossary. [online] Available at: https://www.nlpworld.co.uk/nlp-glossary/n/nominalization/ [Accessed 18 Mar. 2019].

Nlp-mentor.(n.d.). Nominalizations - Recipe for Misunderstanding. [online] Available at: https://nlp-mentor.com/nominalizations/ [Accessed 18 Mar. 2019].

Hall, M. (2010). The Power that Drives "Modal Operators" Meta-States |. [online] Available at: https://www.neurosemantics.com/the-power-that-drives-modal-operators-meta-states/ [Accessed 18 Mar. 2019].

Microdot.net. (n.d.). Modal Operators in the Meta Model. [online] Available at: http://www.microdot.net/nlp/precise-communication/meta-model-8.shtml [Accessed 18 Mar. 2019].

Microdot.net. (n.d.). Modal Operator of Possibility in the Meta Model. [online] Available at: http://www.microdot.net/nlp/precise-communication/meta-model-9.shtml [Accessed 18 Mar.2019].

Nlpnow.com. (2007). NLP Now - Surface Structure Deep Structure - Phillip Holt's World. [online] Available at: http://nlpnow.com/2007/05/nlp-now-surface-structure-deep-structure/ [Accessed 18 Mar. 2019].

Nliblog.com. (n.d.). Linguistic Presuppositions - NLI Blog. [online] Available at: http://nliblog.com/wiki/knowledge-base-2/nlp-2-neurolinguistic-programming/linguistic-presuppositions/ [Accessed 18 Mar. 2019].

Microdot.net. (n.d.). Presuppositions in the Meta Model. [online] Available at: http://www.microdot.net/nlp/precise-communication/meta-model-6.shtml [Accessed 18 Mar. 2019].

Nlpnotes.com. (n.d.). Universal Quantifiers - NLP NotesNLP Notes. [online] Available at: http://nlpnotes.com/language-universal-quantifiers/ [Accessed 18 Mar. 2019].

Crowe-associates.co.uk. (n.d.). NLP

ANCHORING TECHNIQUE | Crowe Associates. [online] Available at: https://www.crowe-associates.co.uk/coaching-and-mentoring-skills/nlp-anchoring-technique/ [Accessed 18 Mar. 2019].

Nlp-secrets.com. (n.d.). Anchoring - NLP Techniques:: NLP-Secrets.com. [online] Available at: https://www.nlp-secrets.com/nlp-technique-anchoring.php [Accessed 18 Mar. 2019].

Crowe-associates.co.uk. (2013). 1507_NLP-Anchoring-Techniques-pdf. [PDF] Available at: http://www.crowe-associates.co.uk/wp-content/uploads/2013/01/1507_NLP-Anchoring-Techniques.pdf [Accessed 18 Mar. 2019].

Trans4mind.com. (n.d.). NLP Anchoring. [online] Available at: https://trans4mind.com/personal_development/mindMastery/anchoring.htm [Accessed 18 Mar. 2019].

Pesch, J. (2018). Anchoring: Visual, Auditory, & Kinesthetic * James Pesch. [online] Available at: https://jamespesch.com/anchoring-visual-auditory-kinesthetic/ [Accessed 18 Mar. 2019].

Excellenceassured.com. (n.d.). NLP Preferred Representational Systems Test. [online] Available at: https://excellenceassured.com/nlp-training/nlp-preferred-representational-systems-test [Accessed 18 Mar. 2019].

Carroll, M. (2011). Making Sense of the World - NLP | NLP Academy. [online] Available at: https://www.nlpacademy.co.uk/articles/view/making_sense_of_the_world_nlp/ [Accessed 18 Mar. 2019].

Mindtools.co.th. (2018). NLP Representational Systems | Mind Tools - Tools for your Mind. [online] Available at: https://www.mindtools.co.th/personal-development/neuro-linguistic-programming/nlp-representational-systems/ [Accessed 18 Mar. 2019].

Schneider, N. (2011). The 4th Perceptual Position in NLP. [online] Available at: https://www.globalnlptraining.com/blog/the-4th-perceptual-position-of-nlp/ [Accessed 18 Mar. 2019].

Hoag, J. (n.d.). NLP Perceptual Positions, by John David Hoag. [online] Available at: http://www.nlpls.com/articles/perceptualPositions.php [Accessed 18 Mar. 2019].

Nlpu.com. (n.d.). NLPU 100 Perceptual Positions. [PDF] Available at: http://www.nlpu.com/FoundationSample/NLPU100Doc/NLPU%20100%20Perceptual%20Positions-s.pdf [Accessed 18 Mar. 2019].

Dilts, R. (1998). Article of the Month Page. [online] Available at: http://www.nlpu.com/Articles/artic21.htm [Accessed 18 Mar. 2019].

Schneider, N. (2011). NLP Perceptual Positions: Fourth Position. [online] Available at: https://www.globalnlptraining.com/blog/nlp-perceptual-positions-4th-position/ [Accessed 18 Mar. 2019].

Mindtrainingsystem.com. (2016). NLP Technique - Perceptual Positions | Mind Training | Mind Training Systems | Mind Training Systems. [online] Available at: http://www.mindtrainingsystems.com/content/nlp-technique-perceptual-positions [Accessed 18 Mar. 2019].

Nlp-now-co-uk. (n.d.). NLP and Rapport - Pegasus NLP. [online] Available at: https://nlp-now.co.uk/nlp-and-rapport/ [Accessed 18 Mar. 2019].

Excellenceassured.com. (n.d.). NLP Mirroring (and Matching) | NLP Rapport. [online] Available at: https://excellenceassured.com/nlp-training/nlp-certification/mirroring [Accessed 18 Mar. 2019].

Excellenceassured.com. (n.d.). NLP Matching | NLP Rapport. [online] Available at: https://excellenceassured.com/nlp-training/nlp-certification/matching [Accessed 18 Mar. 2019].

Nlpworld.co.uk. (n.d.). NLP Mirroring | NLP World - Glossary. [online] Available at: https://www.nlpworld.co.uk/nlp-glossary/m/mirroring/ [Accessed 18 Mar. 2019].

Psychologytoday.com. (n.d.). Neuro-Linguistic Programming Therapy | Psychology Today. [online] Available at: https://www.psychologytoday.com/intl/therapy-types/neuro-linguistic-programming-therapy [Accessed 18 Mar. 2019].

Depressionalliance.org. (n.d.). The DA Guide to Neuro-Linguistic Programming - Depression Alliance. [online] Available at: https://www.depressionalliance.org/neuro-linguistic-programming/ [Accessed 18 Mar. 2019].

Beigntherock.com. (n.d.). NLP for Depression and Anxiety: An Alternative Intervention | Beingthetrock. [online] Available at: http://beingtherock.com/nlp-for-depression-

and-anxiety/ [Accessed 18 Mar. 2019].

Steinhouse, R. (n.d.). Getting Over Depression: Can NLP Keep the Black Dog at Bay? - NLP School. [online] Available at: https://www.nlpschool.com/blog/getting-over-depression-can-nlp-keep-the-black-dog-at-bay/ [Accessed 18 Mar. 2019].

Benalbertscompany.co.az. (n.d.). ADHD in Children can be Treated with NLP | Ben Alberts. [online] Available at: http://www.benalbertscompany.co.za/adhd-children-can-treated-nlp/ [Accessed 18 Mar. 2019].

Adhdcenterforsuccess. (2012). NLP Meets ADHD | ADHD Center for Success. [online] Available at: https://adhdcenterforsuccess.com/site/nlp-meets-adhd/ [Accessed 18 Mar. 2019].

Nimh.nih.gov. (n.d.). NIMH >> Attention-Deficit/Hyperactivity Disorder. [online] Available at: https://www.nimh.nih.gov/health/topics/attenti

on-deficit-hyperactivity-disorder-adhd/index.shtml [Accessed 18 Mar. 2019].

Fettlegenie.com. (2014). How does Neuro Linguistic Programming help in the treatment of ADHD? | Fettle Genie. [online] Available at: http://fettlegenie.com/blog/how-does-neuro-linguistic-programming-help-in-the-treatment-of-adhd/ [Accessed 18 Mar. 2019].

Bolstad, R. & Hamblett, M. (n.d.). Healing The War Within - Transformations NLP. [online] Available at: http://www.transformations.net.nz/trancescript/healing-the-war-within.html [Accessed 18 Mar. 2019].

The-secret-of-mindpower-and-nlp.com. (n.d.). OCD Treatment. [online] Available at: https://www.the-secret-of-mindpower-and-nlp.com/OCD-treatment.html [Accessed 18 Mar. 2019].

Cumberland, A. (n.d.). 5 Ways How Hypnotherapy & NLP Can Cure OCD -

Cumberland Hypnotherapy. [online] Available at: http://www.cumberlandhypnotherapy.co.uk/5-ways-hypnotherapy-nlp-can-cure-ocd/ [Accessed 18 Mar. 2019].

Calmpreneur.com. (n.d.). Can Using NLP Make You More Successful? * Calmpreneur. [online] Available at: https://calmpreneur.com/nlp-successful/ [Accessed 18 Mar. 2019].

Nlp-techniques.org. (n.d.). NLP Career | Developing our Network. [online] Available at: https://www.nlp-techniques.org/what-is-nlp/business/nlp-career/developing-network/ [Accessed 18 Mar. 2019].

Thecoachingroom.com.au. (2018) How to use NLP to unearth your true leadership potential [online] Available at: https://www.thecoachingroom.com.au/blog/how-to-use-nlp-to-unearth-your-true-leadership-potential [Accessed 18 Mar. 2019].

James, A. (n.d.). Barack Obama's Elements of

Charisma. [online] Available at: https://www.nlpcoaching.com/elements-of-charisma-in-barrack-obamas-political-speeches/ [Accessed 18 Mar. 2019].

Excellenceassured.com. (n.d.). Sales training and NLP. [online] Available at: https://excellenceassured.com/2198/selling-and-nlp [Accessed 18 Mar. 2019].

Rea, N. (n.d.). Why is NLP useful for HR Professionals? - NLP World. [online] Available at: https://www.nlpworld.co.uk/why-is-nlp-useful-for-hr-professionals/ [Accessed 18 Mar. 2019].

Unleashyourpotential.org.uk. (n.d.). CBT, NLP & Counselling - what's the different? [online] Available at: https://unleashyourpotential.org.uk/wellbeing-cbt-nlp-whats-difference/ [Accessed 18 Mar. 2019].

Gray, R. & Bourke, F. (n.d.). NLP and CBT | Contemporary Psychotherapy. [online] Available at: http://www.contemporarypsychotherapy.org/volume-6-no-1-summer-2014/nlp-and-cbt/ [Accessed 18 Mar. 2019].

Sharma, M. (2019). CBT and NLP - Two Sides of the Same Coin? - ICHARDS - Institute of Clinical Hypnosis And Related Sciences. [online] Available at: https://www.instituteofclinicalhypnosis.com/cbt-and-nlp-two-sides-of-the-same-coin/ [Accessed 18 Mar. 2019].

Msyaming.com. (n.d.). The Differences Between Cbt, Nlp, and Counselling | MSYAMING. [online] Available at: http://www.msyaming.com/archives/23242 [Accessed 18 Mar. 2019].

Iliades, C. (n.d.). Cognitive-Behavioral Therapy: Is CBT Right for You? - Depression Center - Everyday Health. [online] Available at: https://www.everydayhealth.com/depression/is-cbt-right-for-you-5428.aspx [Accessed 18 Mar.

2019].

West, K. (n.d.). Why Choose Cognitive Behavioral Therapy? | Hope Counselling. [online] Available at: https://hopecounselingeap.com/why-choose-cognitive-behavioral-therapy/ [Accessed 18 Mar. 2019].

Mind.org.uk. (n.d.). Is CBT for me? | Mind, the mental health charity - help for mental health problems. [online] Available at: https://www.mind.org.uk/information-support/drugs-and-treatments/cognitive-behavioural-therapy-cbt/is-cbt-for-me/#.XI_vtyj7TIV [Accessed 18 Mar. 2019].

Carroll, L. (2016). Is CBT the Right Therapy for You? [online] Available at: https://welldoing.org/article/is-cbt-right-therapy-for-you [Accessed 18 Mar. 2019].

Nationalcounsellingsociety.org (n.d.). Types of Therapy. [online] Available at: https://www.nationalcounsellingsociety.org/find-counsellor/types-of-therapy/ [Accessed 18 Mar.

2019].

Drmatt.com. (2012). NLP vs. Hypnosis - What is the difference? - Dr. Matt James. [online] Available at: http://www.drmatt.com/2012/08/10/what-is-the-difference-between-nlp-vs-hypnosis/ [Accessed 18 Mar. 2019].

Livingston, K. (2010). What's The Difference Between Hypnosis & NLP? [online] Available at: http://www.hypnosis101.com/hypnosis-tips/hypnosis-nlp/ [Accessed 18 Mar. 2019].

Cogbtherapy.com. (2014). Introduction to Mindfulness from a DBT Perspective - Cognitive Behavioral Therapy Los Angeles. [online] Available at: http://cogbtherapy.com/cbt-blog/mindfulness-in-dbt [Accessed 18 Mar. 2019].

Cayoun, B. & Elbourne, K. (n.d.). Mindfulness-integrated Cognitive Behaviour Therapy | Tools | Videos. [online] Available at: https://mindfulness.worldsecuresystems.com/w

hat-is-micbt.html [Accessed 18 Mar. 2019].

Webber, C. (2016). How a raisin can help you with mindfulness. [online] Available at: https://www.netdoctor.co.uk/healthy-living/wellbeing/news/a27040/easy-raisin-mindfulness-exercise/ [Accessed 18 Mar. 2019].

Positivepsychologyprogram,com. (2017). 22 Mindfulness Exercises, Techniques & Activities For Adults (+ PDF's). [online] Available at: https://positivepsychologyprogram.com/mindfulness-exercises-techniques-activities/ [Accessed 18 Mar. 2019].

Micbtforwellbeing.com. (n.d.). The Four Steps | Mindfulness-integrated CBT for Wellbeing and Personal Growth |Mindfulness-integrated CBT. [online] Available at: http://www.micbtforwellbeing.com/the-four-steps/ [Accessed 18 Mar. 2019].

Bundrant, M. (n.d.). NLP Swish Pattern ~What Makes it Work and Why it Fails ~. [online] Available at: https://inlpcenter.org/swish-pattern-nlp/ [Accessed 18 Mar. 2019].

Nlp-techniques.org. (n.d.). NLP Technique | Swish. [online] Available at: https://www.nlp-techniques.org/what-is-nlp/swish/ [Accessed 18 Mar. 2019].

Personal-development-planet.com. (n.d.). NLP Swish Pattern - How To Do It! [online] Available at: https://www.personal-development-planet.com/nlp-swish-pattern.html [Accessed 18 Mar. 2019].

Psychologytoday.com. (n.d.). Rational Emotive Behavior Therapy. [online] Available at: https://www.psychologytoday.com/us/therapy-types/rational-emotive-behavior-therapy [Accessed 18 Mar. 2019].

Grieger, R. (2013). Unconditional Self-Acceptance | Psychology Today. [online] Available at: https://www.psychologytoday.com/us/blog/happiness-purpose/201302/unconditional-self-acceptance [Accessed 18 Mar. 2019].

Cherry, K. (2019). The Bandwagon Effect as a Cognitive Bias. [online] Available at: https://www.verywellmind.com/what-is-the-bandwagon-effect-2795895 [Accessed 18 Mar. 2019].

Logicallyfallacious.com. (n.d.). Gambler's Fallacy. [online] Available at: https://www.logicallyfallacious.com/tools/lp/Bo/LogicalFallacies/98/Gambler-s-Fallacy [Accessed 18 Mar. 2019].

Valentine, N. (2016). The gambler's fallacy - explained. [online] Available at: https://www.thecalculatorsite.com/articles/finance/the-gamblers-fallacy.php [Accessed 18 Mar. 2019].

www.ingramcontent.com/pod-product-compliance
Lightning Source LLC
Chambersburg PA
CBHW030108100526
44591CB00009B/328